CU00924225

The Batsford Book of
LAMPSHADES

The Batsford Book of
LAMPSHADES

ANGELA FISHBURN

B.T. Batsford London

For Michael

Acknowledgements

My thanks are due to Jackie Allen for all the illustrations and to Alma Rafter for her colour photographs. I should also like to thank Katie Beckett for her help in reading the typescript and all my students who kindly lent me lampshades and bases for the photographs, and The Upstairs Shop who lent the lampshade for the photograph between pages 48 and 49.

The author and publishers would like to thank Sanderson & Son Ltd for their permission to reproduce their photograph on the front jacket and Crown Wallcoverings for their permission to reproduce their photograph on the back jacket.

First published 1984
© Angela Fishburn 1984

All rights reserved. No part of this publication may be reproduced in any form or by any means without permission from the Publishers

ISBN 0 7134 2862 7

Photoset in Monophoto Bembo by
Servis Filmsetting Ltd, Manchester
Printed in Great Britain by
The Anchor Press Ltd, Tiptree, Essex
for the publishers,
B.T. Batsford Ltd,
4 Fitzhardinge Street,
London, W1H 0AH

Contents

Introduction

Lampshade-making is a creative craft which has become very popular during recent years. It is a most satisfying and rewarding pastime, and for those who enjoy making things for the home, it is a skill worth acquiring.

It is not always easy to find ready-made lampshades that match or co-ordinate well with other furnishings and if they can be found, they are usually rather costly. However, it is often possible to make attractive shades from fabric remaining over from other soft furnishing projects and thereby create an original scheme.

Lampshades play an important part in the appearance of a room, for they are accessories that are both functional and decorative. Because they take very little fabric they are comparatively inexpensive to make and can therefore be changed more frequently, perhaps, than other soft furnishings. Fresh lampshades give a lift to a room if chosen and made with care. They also provide an opportunity for the expert and the beginner alike to combine and use their other skills, for example fabric painting and dyeing, patchwork and quilting, as well as lace and other crafts.

A lampshade demands a high standard of workmanship and meticulous attention to detail, because as soon as it is lit, any defects will immediately become apparent.

Fashions in lampshades are always changing, and with the introduction of new designs and fabrics a fresh challenge is constantly presented.

ONE
Lighting in the home

Lighting the home is very important and many factors need to be considered before a choice is made.

Firstly, the lighting must be safe and convenient, and must suit the functions of the room. Adequate light for study, sewing, cooking, etc. must be provided. We have progressed a long way since the days of oil lamps and candles, although these are still sometimes adapted to suit modern designs. Make sure that enough electrical points are provided and that they are well positioned for the light to be effective. Bad lighting is not only dangerous but can make a room look dismal and unwelcoming and can cause eye strain and accidents. It is therefore important to take into account the positions and intensity of the light required in each part of the living space, carefully considering both the functional and aeshetic needs of each area.

Lighting brings a home to life because colour is only present when there is light. Colours and textures are, moreover, affected by the degree of light available. An object seen in sunlight looks quite different from that seen in candlelight because the intensity of the light being reflected from the object's surface is different, so the colour appears to vary. It follows that the textures of soft furnishing fabrics, pictures, decorative and other objects in the home, can be emphasised or subdued by the use of

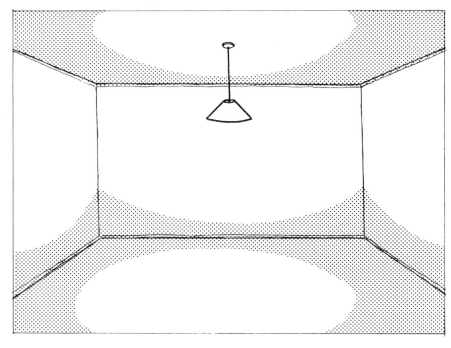

Fig. 1 *Central hanging light gives just one pool of light*

9

Fig. 2 *Good lighting is necessary above or at the sides of a mirror. Choose light colours for lampshades at the side of a bed as these may be needed for reading*

carefully chosen lighting. A light can be warm or cool, high or low, depending on the method and type of lighting and fittings used.

Design and colour

Choose fittings for lighting carefully, making sure that the fitting will be aesthetically pleasing as well as functional. Avoid over-fussy, complicated designs that can so easily distract the eye from a beautifully made silk or cotton shade. Choose a simple design in alabaster, brass or ceramics and make the lampshade to complement it.

There is more to making lampshades than just covering the frame and there are various ways of making them, but before deciding which to choose bear in mind the following points:

(1) A lampshade is an important focal point in a room – it is often illuminated, and that alone will draw attention to it. Lampshades can be made in bold colours to fit into contemporary modern schemes – they play an important role here – and their colours and designs must fit in well with the overall decor.

(2) If possible plan the lighting scheme as a whole, so that all the lampshades in the room balance and tone well together. For example, in a large room use one or two large bases with large lampshades to complement them. Small bases with tiny shades look inappropriate in this situation and do nothing to add to the feeling of space.

(3) One of the most important functions of a lampshade is to give adequate lighting for its purpose. It must therefore be attractive and effective when lit, but it must also fit into the decorative scheme during the day, when it is not illuminated.

(4) Colour has great power and reflects our personality, as is shown in the clothes that we wear. It is also evident in the home, where different colours reflect different moods. Similarly with lampshades – some colours are thought to be more suitable or restful than others.

(5) Lighting at night will change the overall tone and emphasis of a room, and it is therefore important to place lighting as effectively as possible (*figs 1–6*). Light from a lampshade is also affected by its colour and texture.

(6) It is usually more effective to have several sources of light in a room rather than one central hanging light. Several pools of light, shining up or down, make a room more interesting.

(7) Try to use pale colours for lampshades that are to be used for reading, e.g. at a bedside or in a study, so that the maximum amount of light is obtained. Darker colours can be used elsewhere in the room for their dramatic effect.

(8) A naked bulb should be covered to avoid glare, except in the case of low wattage candle bulbs and chandelier-type fittings. With chandeliers, clear bulbs should be used, not pearl ones, for these would spoil the effect of the crystal in the chandelier.

Choosing a base

A large selection of bases is available; they come in various shapes and sizes, so that it is often difficult to know which one to choose. But it is important that the lampshade be in proportion to the base and balances well. Try to match the line of the frame to the base so that the two together present a pleasing design of good proportions (*fig.* 7). As a general guide, a shade should be approximately two-thirds the height of the base and the diameter of the bottom of the shade approximately that of the height of the base.

If possible, buy the base first and then choose a lampshade frame to suit it. This is sometimes easier said than done, but it is well worth the trouble of taking the base to the shop to choose a suitable frame.

Some very good ceramic and alabaster bases are obtainable nowadays – some in chain stores. They

Fig. 3 *Several sources of light make a room more interesting*

Opposite above and below
Fig. 4 *Florescent tubes over work surfaces or spot lights on the ceiling give practical light in a kitchen. A pretty lampshade over the dining area enhances the practical scheme*

Fig. 5 *Make sure halls and stairs and dark corridors are well lit to avoid accidents*

Fig. 6 *Provided there is a good light over or at both sides of the mirror a decorative lampshade can be used on the ceiling*

are well worth looking for. Make sure that the base is firm and does not tip over easily. (If necessary, weight the base by filling it with sand.) Choose plain bases with simple designs and avoid fussy ones with too much detail.

Old brass candlesticks make good bases for lampshades and can be converted at specialist shops. Reproduction ones are also obtainable and can look very elegant. Elegant old vases can sometimes be found in antique or junk shops, and even if slightly damaged can make attractive bases for lampshades. The cost of converting these varies with the method and materials used and it is advisable to obtain an estimate before the work is undertaken.

It is seldom worth using wine decanters and bottles for lamp bases; they are not usually of the right proportions for bases, mainly because of their narrow necks. Carboys, however, make very attractive bases for larger shades and can be filled with pebbles, plants, etc. to make an arresting, decorative feature.

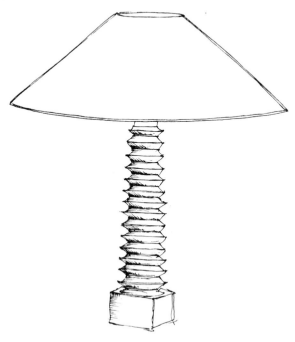

Fig. 7 *Lampshade styles and bases*

Fig. 7 *Continued*

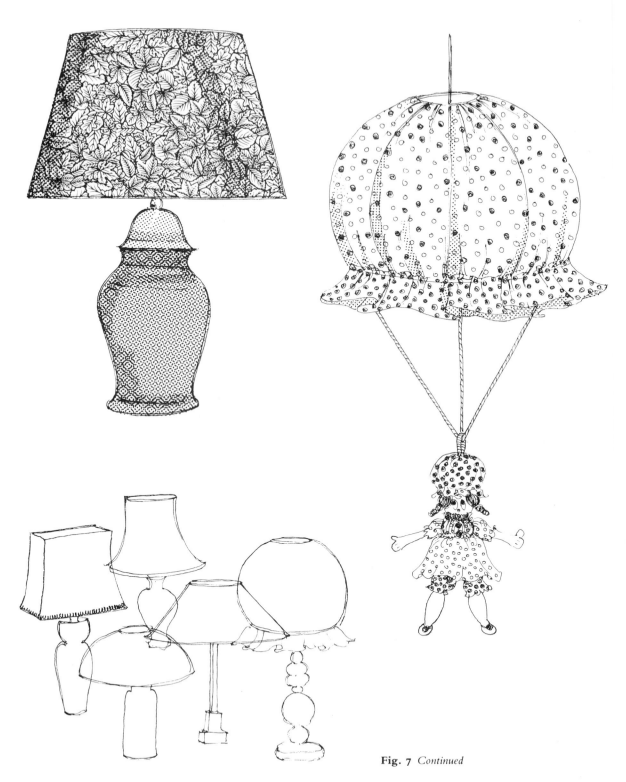

Fig. 7 *Continued*

TWO
Fabrics for lampshades

Choose fabrics for lampshades carefully, taking into consideration colour, texture and effect. If the main purpose of the lampshade is to provide a good light, select translucent fabrics such as crepe de Chine, silks and fine cottons. These are best lined with crepe-backed satin, which will give body to the shade and reflect the light well.

Before choosing fabric for lampshades, collect samples and cuttings in different colours and textures. Experiment with them in different combinations to see whether they tone or contrast well with the rest of the decorative scheme. Test the fabrics over a lighted bulb to see the effect produced. It is quite a good idea to take a torch when buying lampshade fabric, and test the fabric in the shop.

Remember also, when choosing lampshade fabric, that colour creates illusions of shape and size. A pale colour will make the lampshade appear larger than if a darker tone is used. Pale colours permit more light than prints or darker colours, too, and this must be remembered when making a lampshade for reading or for study.

Coloured linings can be used very effectively under broderie anglaise and other pale coloured fabrics. Coloured linings can be used under white fabrics to give warmth to an otherwise cold light. It is worth experimenting with both lining and cover fabrics before making a choice.

Remain aware of current trends and fashions by looking at the lighting departments of large shops and stores. Keep a scrapbook and collect pictures of ideas and colour combinations. This is invaluable for ideas which may otherwise be lost or forgotten.

When choosing fabrics for soft lampshades (see pages 31 and 60 for difference between soft and firm lampshades) bear in mind the following points and do not be afraid to experiment with new man-made fabrics as they become available, provided they appear to have the necessary qualities.

(1) Use fabric that has plenty of 'give' or elasticity. Fabric that stretches well will mould easily to the shape of the frame without wrinkling. Rigid, non-stretchy fabrics are not suitable for curved or bowed empire shapes. Use crepe de Chine, silks, shantung, wild silk, fine cottons or crepe-backed satin for making tailored shades.

(2) Fabrics that split and tear easily are not suitable, e.g. taffeta, rayon and satin dress lining fabrics, for these show up all pin marks and do not wash well.

(3) Dress cottons, ginghams, polyester/cotton sheeting, broderie anglaise, lace and lawn are particularly suitable for tiffany-style lampshades, and coloured linings can be used effectively with some of these fabrics.

(4) When choosing patterned fabrics, bear in mind that small designs are usually the most suitable on small frames, as large patterns can lose their impact and do not show up to advantage.

(5) Heavy furnishing fabrics and cottons and materials that do not stretch well are not suitable for lampshades. Besides being difficult to work, they permit very little light to filter through the fabric and the shade will be too opaque. Some fabrics are not attractive when put over a light, e.g. brocades, and some velvets, so test these carefully first.

(6) Horizontally and vertically striped fabric can cause problems when making up. It can be very difficult indeed to match stripes except when they are used for a hard drum shade or are positioned diagonally.

(7) When making pleated lampshades choose fabric with good draping qualities such as silk chiffon, georgette and silk shantung. Dress cottons, poly/cotton sheeting, voile and some furnishing cottons can also be used for pleating, but check first to see that the finished result will not be too bulky.

(8) Avoid inflammable fabrics such as nylons and some of te man-made fabrics.

(9) Use crepe-backed satin for lining soft lampshades. It is a fabric that stretches well and gives body to the shade when lightweight fabrics are used for the cover; moreover, its shiny surface reflects the light well. Alternatively, choose shantung silk or a suitable man-made fabric that stretches well.

(10) Any colour is acceptable for a lampshade provided it enhances the decorative scheme and fulfils its functions properly. However, when il-luminated, some colours give a more attractive light than others. Good colours include tones of yellow and pink. All white shades give a cold, hard light but can be given a hint of warmth if lined with pale pink or peach colour. Light bulbs, too, can be obtained in a variety of shapes and colours, and can give a very pleasant soft light when used with these shades. Blue lampshades produce a cold light; browns and greens can be effective, but tend to give a dingy light, so care is needed when using them. If in doubt, try the fabrics first over a lighted bulb and experiment with different coloured linings.

(11) Choose fabrics that have good washing qualities, for lampshades can be washed successfully if treated with care (see page 88).

(12) Patchwork, quilting and appliqué are some of the crafts that can be employed when making lampshades. Lace and crochet can also be used to good effect, and for those with artistic talent much can be done to decorate shades in an original way.

Linings

Linings play an important part in the construction of a lampshade and are used for a number of reasons. The main functions of linings are:

(1) To conceal the struts and framework of the shade, particularly in a pendant (hanging) shade.

(2) To prevent the bulb from showing through the cover fabric. It should not be possible to see the outline of the bulb when lit.

(3) To give body to the shade when using lightweight or open-work fabrics such as pure silk chiffon, lace and voile.

(4) To reflect as much light as possible. A shiny white lining reflects the maximum amount of light. Cream, peach and pink linings give a warmer glow.

(5) To obtain different effects by using coloured linings under white or pale coloured outer covers.

There are three main methods of lining lampshades:

1 Balloon lining
This is fitted inside the struts on the inside of the frame and needs practice to make perfectly. It is fitted after the cover has been sewn to the outside of the frame. This type of lining is used wherever possible, as it conceals all the struts and framework. However, it is not possible to use it on all frames, e.g. tiffany-style frames and some square and rectangular ones. These should have an external lining, or a lining made using the sectional method (see page 55).

2 External lining
This is fitted on to the outer side of the struts where a balloon lining is not practical. It applies to small chandelier-type shades and to wall lights where a baloon lining would be too close to the bulb for safety. An external lining is also used on square and tiffany-style frames as the shape of these makes a balloon lining impossible. A slight variation of this lining is used when making pleated and swathed lampshades (see page 47).

3 Pleated lining
Sometimes a lampshade may need a pleated lining and these can be very attractive when used on coolie shades or fluted drum shades. When this type of lining is used in a pleated lampshade, it is important to make sure that both sets of pleating coincide, or a bad effect will result.

There is a wide range of fabrics on the market suitable for lampshade making, but some are easier to handle than others. Fabrics fall into two cate-gories: natural and man-made. Natural fibres are based on raw materials from animal and vegetable sources; man-made fibres are those manufactured by chemically treating raw materials such as minerals and vegetables.

Natural fibres

Silk Silk is the fine thread which is reeled from the cocoon of the silkworm larva, then wound on bobbins to be woven into fabric. It is manufactured mainly in the East, although France has long been renowned as the centre of silk manufacture in Europe. Silk is expensive to produce, as the insects which spin the fibres are costly to rear. It has great strength but is weakened by strong sunlight. Silk is a luxury fabric. It dyes extremely well, and many subtle colours can be obtained. It washes well and has a natural lustre which reflects the light, making it an ideal choice for lampshade making.

Cotton The cotton plant is a flowering shrub whose yellow blooms become covered with tufts of cotton wool. This is picked, carded and spun to produce cotton thread and fabric. Cotton is strong and hard-wearing, washes well and can be easily printed and dyed.

Man-made fibres

Great developments have recently taken place in the manufacture of man-made fibres, and progress is constantly being made in this field. New processes and techniques have improved the properties of the fabrics and it is now very difficult to distinguish them from the natural fibres which they imitate.

Man-made fibres are produced by chemically treating basic raw materials such as wood pulp, petroleum extracts, by-products of coal, casein, cotton linters and groundnuts. Most of the fabrics produced are not absorbent and tend to look dirty rather quickly. This is because the dirt stays on the surface and is not absorbed by the fabric. However, this fact makes them easy to clean. Most synthetic fibres can be blended with natural fibres or other man-made fibres to produce fabrics with varying uses and finishes, strengths and resilience. Some man-made fibres melt if subjected to high tempera-tures and this must be borne in mind when choosing fabrics for lampshades. It is necessary to make quite sure that the fabric will not be too close to the bulb and that a sufficiently low wattage bulb is used for the size of lampshade frame.

1 Crepe-backed satin
Originally made in rayon but now also produced in man-made fibres, this is a good choice for the beginner as well as for the more experienced, as it is the easiest of all fabrics to use. It stretches well, is reasonably priced and is available in a good range of colours. It can be used for making both the cover and the lining of the lampshade and can be used either on the crepe or the satin side to good effect. It is the best choice for all linings and is particularly suitable for curved shapes where 'stretch' is of vital importance.

2 Dupion
This is an attractive fabric suitable for lampshade covers and has the appearance of slubbed silk. It is mostly made from man-made fibres, but is available in a very wide range of subtle colours. It is reasonably priced and is best used in the light colours for little light filters through most of the darker colours, which give a drab and dingy light. As this fabric frays badly, generous seam allowances should be made.

3 Jap silk
Although this is a suitable fabric for lining small shades, it is not satisfactory when used on larger frames as it pin-marks easily and can split when stretched if great care is not taken. It is, however, reasonably priced and washes well.

4 Silk shantung
This is a good choice of fabric for both outer covers and linings. It is produced in a limited range of colours, is reasonably priced and washes well. It is suitable for both large and small shades and is easy to handle.

5 Wild silk
This is a luxury fabric that has a most attractive natural grain and shimmer which other materials lack. As this fabric dyes so well it is available in a

very subtle range of colours, all of which seem ideally suited to lampshades. It is strong, easy to handle and washes well. It is a very versatile fabric, suitable for all sizes of lampshades.

6 Silk chiffon

This is the best choice of fabric when making traditional-style pleated or swathed lampshades. It drapes well and retains the pleating, unlike its man-made counterpart which is too springy for the pleats to lie flat. Silk chiffon is available in a good range of colours and washes extremely well. Cotton chiffon can also be used for pleated or swathed lampshades, and is a more economical choice.

7 Polyester/cotton sheeting

This fabric, made partly from natural cotton fibres and partly from man-made fibres, makes a suitable choice for lampshades. It can be used pleated or plain, washes well and is made in co-ordinating and plain colours and prints.

8 Dress and furnishing cottons

These make delightful covers for lampshades and can match or co-ordinate with other furnishings. Choose from fine lawns, broderie anglaise, ginghams and light furnishing cottons. For best effect when choosing broderie anglaise, select fabrics with small patterns, not large cut-out designs. Light-weight furnishing cottons stretch better than heavier, better quality ones. These do not diffuse the light well and are also difficult to work successfully. Ginghams make up into successful lampshades as they are light in weight and their fresh crisp look is particularly suited to kitchens and bathrooms.

9 Cotton lace

This can be used successfully for lampshades but sometimes needs an interlining as well as a lining, depending on the design. Lace looks very effective when used over a coloured lining and this type of lampshade can be made to match curtains, bedspreads or blinds.

THREE
Frames and fittings

In order to make a successful lampshade it is essential to have a firm, sound frame. It is the foundation on to which the fabric is stretched and sewn and the effort involved is rarely worth it unless a good frame is used. Bent frames result in distorted shades, and struts sometimes come away from the frame if the soldering is weak.

Choose a plastic-coated frame if possible, as these need little or no preparation. They are a little more costly than the uncoated copper or galvanized frames, but last much longer as they are unlikely to become rusty. If a plastic coated frame is not available choose a frame that is made from a copper wire. This should be of a suitable gauge or thickness for the frame, enabling it to support the fabric firmly. File down any rough edges at the joints, as these may push through the binding tape and fabric. Paint the frame with a quick-drying enamel or gloss paint, making sure that this is quite hard before binding with tape. The best frames have soldered wires, but some are spot-welded, so it is wise to check that joints are firm and strong before the frame is purchased. Frames sometimes become badly bent out of shape in the shop, faults which are difficult to remedy.

As long as they are not badly rusted or out of shape, it is often worth re-covering old frames, particularly if they are of a pleasing or unusual design. Carefully take off the old binding tape, and check for rust. File down if necessary, or rub with a fine sandpaper and paint in the usual way.

Frames are made for use with various different types of fittings. Make sure that you choose the correct fitting for the lamp or light in question. Examples of fittings are given in figs 8–26.

Frames are made in sizes from 10 cm (4 in) for

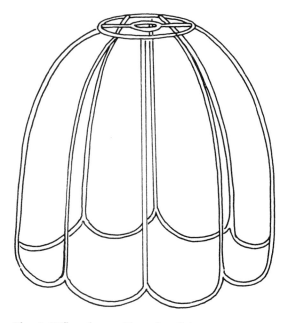

Fig. 8 *Tiffany frame with pendant fitting*

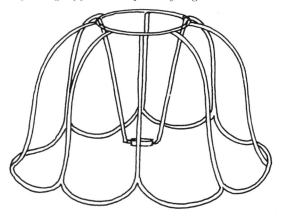

Fig. 9 *Variation of a tiffany style*

small wall lights and chandelier fittings to 51–56 cm (20–22 in) for large lamps. This measurement is taken across the diameter of the base ring.

New shapes and sizes of frame are always being introduced and some exciting designs have appeared recently. When an unusual size or shape of lampshade is required it is sometimes possible to have one made to order by a specialist wire-worker, though these are not easy to find.

Lampshades fall into two groups – soft fabric shades and firm rigid ones. Soft fabric lampshades are made from flexible materials – silks, satins etc. It is essential to make these on frames that have enough struts as well as a ring at the top and bottom, for it is the struts that give the shade its shape.

Firm lampshades are made from stiff or rigid materials such as buckram or card. When making a firm shade, a ring set is used. This consists of a top and bottom ring with the appropriate fitting. Strutted frames can also be used, but struts are not essential as the rigid materials provide the shape of the shade.

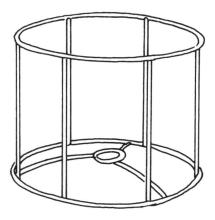

Fig. 10 *Drum frame with dropped pendant fitting*

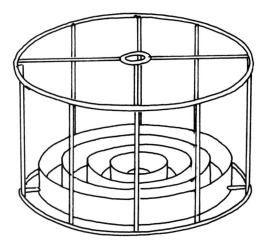

Fig. 12 *Drum frame using a louvre fitting to diffuse the light. Leave at least 2.5 cm (1 in) between bulb and louvre fitting*

Fig. 11 *Bowed empire frame with butterfly clip for small shades and wall lights*

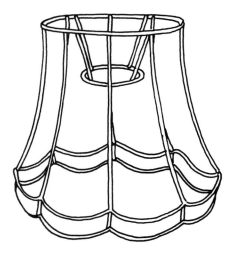

Fig. 13 *Bowed empire frame with a collar and a duplex fitting*

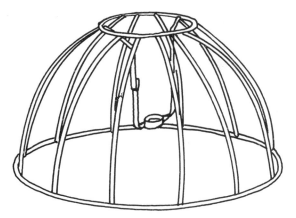

Fig. 14 *Tiffany frame with adjustable gimbal/tilter fitting*

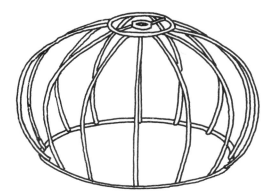

Fig. 15 *Tiffany frame with more struts than 8, 9 or 14. It has very pronounced curves and is best made up by the gathered method*

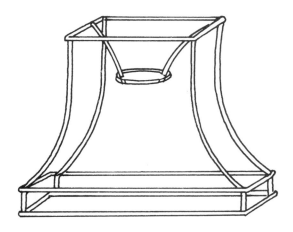

Fig. 16 *Square frame with duplex fitting*

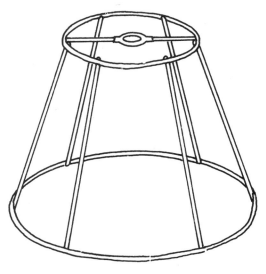

Fig. 17 *Straight-sided empire frame with pendant fitting*

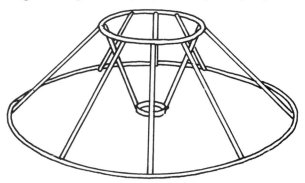

Fig. 18 *Coolie frame with adjustable gimbal/tilter fitting*

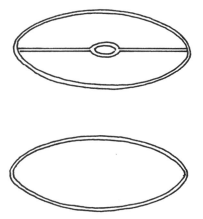

Fig. 19 *Ring set for making firm lampshades*

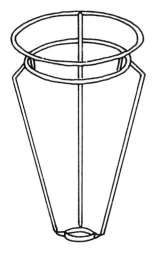

Fig. 20 *Shade carrier or support for duplex fittings*

Fig. 23 *Bowed oval frame with collar*

Fig. 24 *Eight-panel octagon frame*

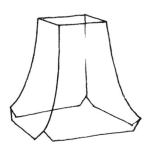

Fig. 21 *Square frame with four panels*

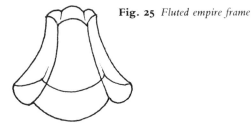

Fig. 25 *Fluted empire frame*

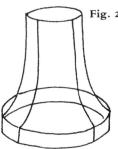

Fig. 26 *Bowed empire frame with collar*

Fig. 22 *Oblong frame*

FOUR
Tools and equipment

Apart from the frame, fabric and trimmings it is not necessary to have any special tools for making lampshades, but the basic equipment listed below will be found useful.

Tools and equipment in the workbox should be in good working order and kept tidily together to be available when needed. Replenish the workbox from time to time with new pins and needles, for rust or corrosion pin-marks expensive fabrics.

When buying new tools, always buy the best quality possible and use them only for the purpose for which they were intended. Never use cutting-out shears for cutting paper – keep them only for needlework. If scissors need sharpening, have them professionally ground or return them to the manufacturer.

Pins
Best quality steel dressmaking pins should be used, first making sure that they are free from rust. Glass-headed pins can be used, but as they are extremely sharp extra care is needed when using them. Correct pinning is an important process in the making of a successful lampshade and poor quality pins can tear the fabric and make marks that cannot easily be removed. Invest in a new pack of steel dressmaking pins, discarding any that are at all rusty, and keep them in the tin or box provided. Never use pins that have dropped on the floor – they collect dust that is not visible to the naked eye. Do not leave pins in fabric longer than necessary as they will mark delicate material if left for long periods.

Needles
Use Sharps 3–9 for making soft lampshades and Betweens 5–6 for firm shades.

Lampshade tape
Use special lampshade tape or a soft, loosely woven unbleached cotton tape that is 1.3 cm ($\frac{1}{2}$ in) wide. This can easily be dyed with a cold water dye to the colour of the lining fabric if required, once the frame has been taped, and is particularly useful on tiffany-style lampshades or on shades where the struts will show.

Adhesive
Use a good quick-drying all-purpose adhesive when making firm lampshades. Use it also when applying certain trimmings to soft lampshades where stitching is not satisfactory, as in the case of velvet ribbon and crossway strip. A small knife or fruit knife is ideal for applying the adhesive.

Clothes pegs
Wooden clip-on clothes pegs with springs are required when making firm lampshades.

Scissors
A sharp pair of scissors 20.5–23 cm (8–9 in) long is required for cutting out, and a smaller pair 12.5–14 cm (5–$5\frac{1}{2}$ in) long for cutting thread, etc. Choose the best quality possible and keep them well sharpened.

Thimble
Choose a metal one to protect te middle finger. Thimbles are particularly important when sewing firm fabric lampshades and coarse materials.

Threads
Match the thread to the fabric where possible. Use a synthetic thread with a synthetic fabric. For general

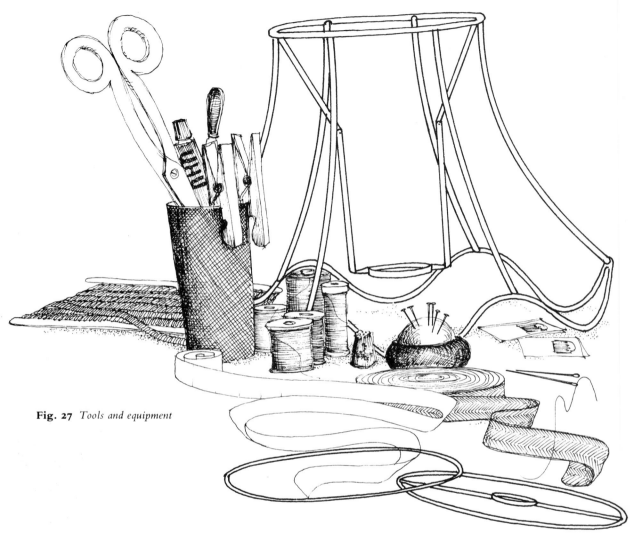

Fig. 27 *Tools and equipment*

use and for medium-weight fabric such as cotton, choose Sylko 40 or 50. Use silk or No. 60 cotton on finer fabrics, and tacking-cotton for basting.

Tape measure
Choose a fibreglass or linen tape with a stiffened end. These are the most reliable as they will not stretch easily.

Quick unpick
This is a small ripping tool used for unpicking seams and stitches and is very useful when making lampshades with balloon linings.

Lampshade frames
These are generally available from good craft and haberdashery shops as well as from some large stores.

Fabrics to cover the frame
(see Chapters 2 and 7).

Trimmings
Good commercial trimmings are readily available but attractive ones can also be made by hand or machine (Chapter 8).

FIVE

Preparation and taping of the frame

Preparation

As most lampshade frames are made from plastic or nylon-coated metal or copper wires little preparation is usually required apart from a wipe over with a duster. Sometimes, however, the plastic has been applied rather thickly, leaving a slight bump which may show through the fabric when the lampshade is on. If necessary, cut off the excess plastic with a sharp knife or file down with a metal file.

When a frame has a tilting gimbal fitting the plastic coating will cover the moving part and it is necessary to cut through the plastic with a sharp knife to enable it to work freely at both sides of the frame on the tilter fitting.

With copper or metal frames check that there are no rough edges that may damage the binding tape or fabric. If necessary, file down with a metal file and paint with a quick-drying gloss or enamel paint. This helps to prevent the frame from rusting.

Taping the frame

This is a most important process, for it provides the firm foundation on which to pin and stitch the fabric. It also helps to prevent rust forming. The tape needs to be firm, smooth and tight on all struts and rings. If it is at all loose the stitching will slip and the finished shade will be loose and baggy and disappointing as a result.

(1) Use 1.3 cm ($\frac{1}{2}$ in) wide lampshade tape, or soft unbleached cotton tape. This latter is a poor quality tape that is loosely woven and off-white in colour. It

is easily dyed with a cold water dye to the colour of the lining, if necessary.

(2) *Paris binding.* This can be used for binding the frame when it is required to match the colour of the lining fabric, e.g. on a tiffany shade. Paris binding is available in a good range of colours.

(3) *Jap silk.* This can be used to bind the struts to obtain a really smooth finish when an un-coated frame is being used. Cut the silk into 2.5 cm (1 in) strips and turn in one raw edge as the strut is bound. Lampshade tape must be used on the struts where pinning or sewing will take place i.e. the top and bottom rings and side struts, as it is not possible to sew or pin onto a strut or ring bound with Jap silk.

(4) *Bias binding.* This is available in a good range of colours. Iron one side open to prevent it from being too bulky.

Quantity of tape

For each strut allow approximately one and a half times its length in tape. If more is allowed the tape will become too bulky.

For the top and bottom rings allow twice the circumference. More is needed for the rings, as the tape is bound round each joint of the strut and ring.

Bind each strut separately and then bind the top and bottom rings. Always start and finish at a joint in the strut in order to prevent the tape from working loose. No sewing is necessary except when taping rings for firm lampshades where there are no struts. In such a case, use a piece of adhesive tape to hold the tape in position when starting. Finish by oversewing the tape on the outside of the ring so that when the fabric or card is applied to the ring it covers the stitching (*fig. 28*).

With plastic-coated frames it is not necessary to bind every strut with tape but the top and bottom rings must be bound, and also any struts where sewing or pinning will take place.

(1) Place the tape under the ring, starting at the top of the frame. Tuck in and wind the tape round the strut, just overlapping it. Pull the tape slightly each time round as this stretches it and makes it mould more easily to the strut. Keep the tape smooth and taut and avoid any ridges that may threaten to appear (*figs 29–35*).

(2) At the bottom of the strut turn the lampshade to the position in fig. 32 and wind the tape round the bottom ring, taking it first to the left and then to the right of the ring (a figure of eight). Finish off with a knot as in fig. 33 and pull tightly. The end of the tape should come from the front of the frame. Trim off the end to the bottom ring. It is not necessary to stitch the end. If it has been bound tightly it will not unwind.

(3) Bind each strut in this way and then bind the top and bottom rings, making a figure of eight round each joint in the strut and ring. Finish off as before.

Fig. 28 *Oversewing the tape into position on the outside edge of the ring*

Figs 29 & **30** *Starting to tape the strut*

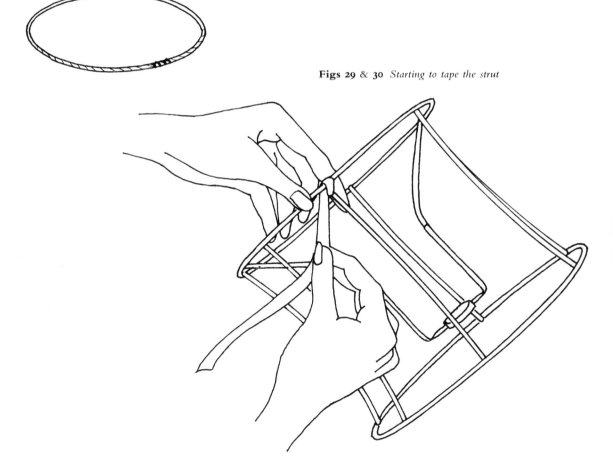

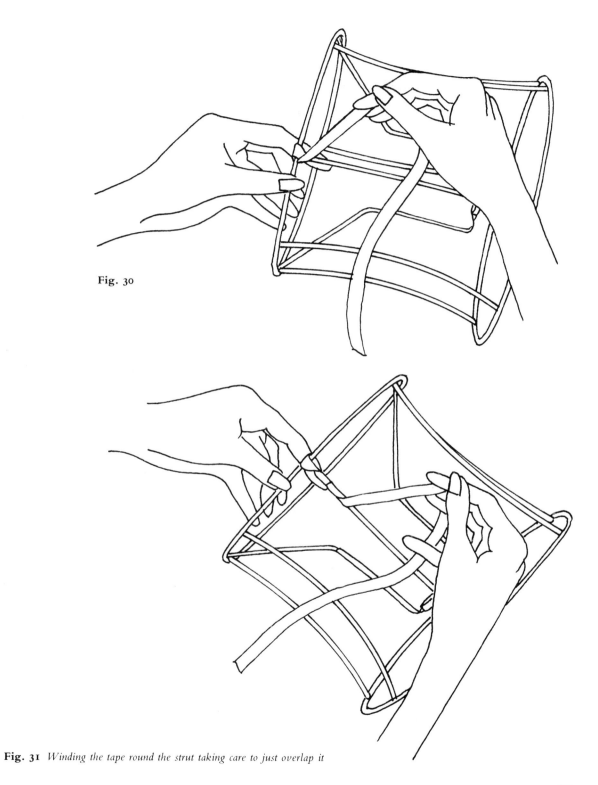

Fig. 30

Fig. 31 *Winding the tape round the strut taking care to just overlap it*

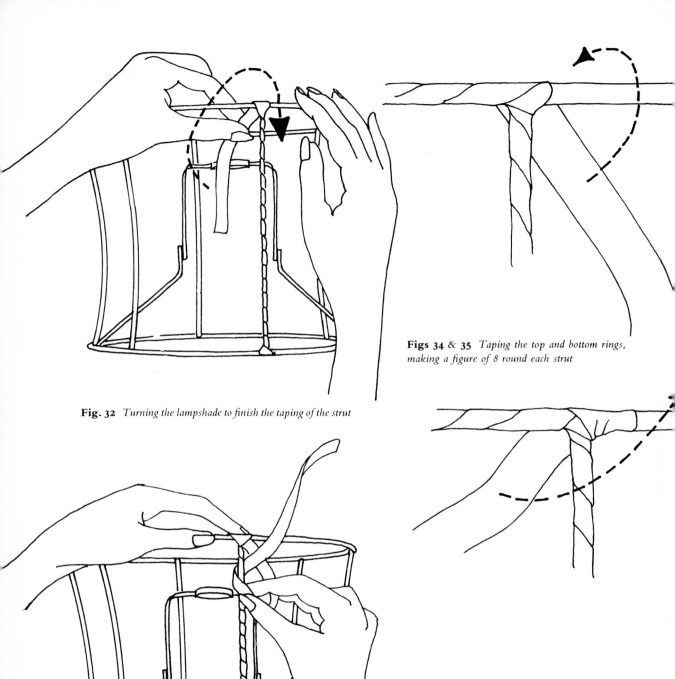

Fig. 32 *Turning the lampshade to finish the taping of the strut*

Figs 34 & 35 *Taping the top and bottom rings, making a figure of 8 round each strut*

Fig. 33 *Finishing the taping at the bottom ring*

SIX

Soft (fabric-covered) lampshades

Classic lampshade with balloon lining

(1) This method of making lampshades can be applied to many soft-fabric shades where the measurement round the middle or smallest part of the frame is not less than that of the top ring. Frames with accentuated waists are more satisfactorily worked in two or more sections depending on their design and size. However, if the measurement of the 'waist' does not vary greatly from that of the top ring this method can safely be used provided the fabric is flexible enough and is worked on the cross grain instead of on the straight grain.

(2) To estimate the amount of fabric needed, measure the depth of the frame plus 10 cm (4 in), and the circumference of the bottom ring (or the largest part of the frame) plus 12.5 cm (5 in). If

Fig. 36 *Fabric placed onto the frame on the straight of the grain*

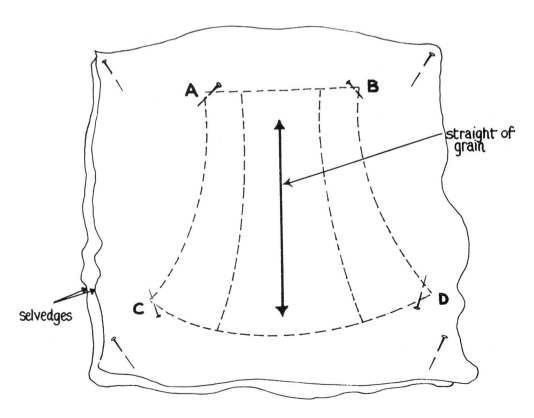

necessary, two pieces of fabric can be cut. For waisted shades the fabric must be cut on the cross grain (see above).

(3) The cover and the lining are prepared in the same way, using double material and pinning on to one half of the frame only. The cover is stitched to the frame first, and the balloon lining is inserted afterwards.

Tailored shades made by this method should, where possible, have the fabric pinned to the frame with the selvedge or straight grain running from the top of the frame to the bottom (*fig. 36*) except as mentioned in (1) above. Fabric stretched on the straight grain springs back to its original position more easily than that stretched on the cross. It is therefore easier to rectify errors in pinning and stretching.

Fig. 37 *Marking the seamline with a pencil. Tacking stitches in position near the pins*

Fitting the fabric to the frame

(1) Tape the frame as described on page 27. Fold the cover fabric in half with the right sides together, and pin to hold in position. Place this on to one side of the frame only, with the straight grain running down the middle of the frame and the selvedges of the material running from the top to the bottom (*fig. 36*).

(2) Place a pin at A B C and D, pinning just into the top of the tape and not through to the back of the frame. Pin the fabric to the two side struts AC and BD, placing pins at 2.5 cm (1 in) intervals. Do not pin at the top and bottom rings until most of the fullness has been taken to the sides. Place pins on the side struts with the heads facing towards the centre of the shade. Pins on the top and bottom rings should face towards the centre, as this reduces the risk of damaging clothes and body (*fig. 37*).

(3) Tighten the fabric at the top and bottom rings to remove wrinkles, pinning at every 2.5 cm (1 in).

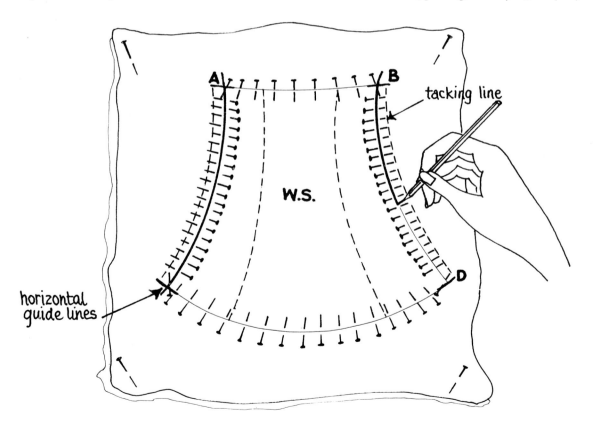

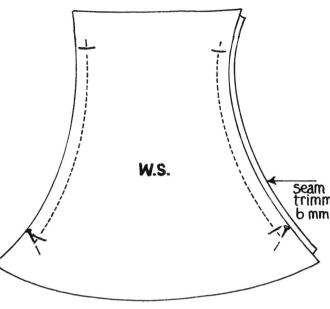

Fig. 38 *Seams machined and trimmed to 6 mm ($\frac{1}{4}$ in)*

(4) Complete the pinning on the side struts, inserting pins first at 1.3 cm ($\frac{1}{2}$ in) intervals and then finally at 6 mm ($\frac{1}{4}$ in).

(5) With a hard pencil, carefully draw a faint line over the pins on the side struts, extending the pencil mark 1.3 cm ($\frac{1}{2}$ in) round the top and bottom rings at A B C and D (*fig. 37*). Tack through the double thickness of fabric about 1.3 cm ($\frac{1}{2}$ in) from the pins on the side struts (*fig. 37*).

(6) Remove all pins from the fabric and machine down the pencil line from the top to the bottom, using a medium-sized stitch and stretching the fabric very slightly while stitching. This prevents the stitches from breaking when the cover is stretched over the top of the frame.

(7) Trim the seams to 6 mm ($\frac{1}{4}$ in) at each side and cut along the fold line if there is one (*fig. 38*).

(8) Prepare the lining in the same way but stitch the seams 3 mm ($\frac{1}{8}$ in) inside the pencil lines. Press flat and set aside.

Fitting the cover

(1) Press the outer cover keeping the fabric flat – do not press the seams open.

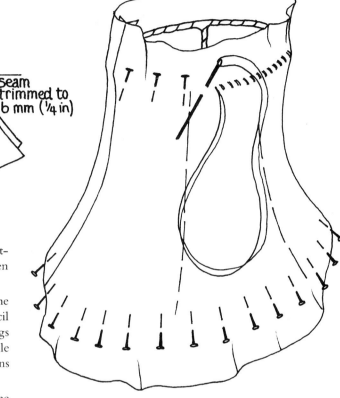

Fig. 39 *Oversewing the cover to the frame working from right to left*

(2) Slip the cover over the frame with the right sides outside, positioning the seams on the side struts. Match the horizontal pencil lines at the top and bottom rings.

(3) Pin the fabric to the top and bottom rings of the frame, making sure that the seams do not slip out of place. Gradually tighten and adjust the fabric so that it fits over the frame well.

(4) Oversew the cover to the frame using a short length of double, matching thread. Do not use a long piece of thread as this will knot easily and catch round the pins. The stitches should be sewn on to

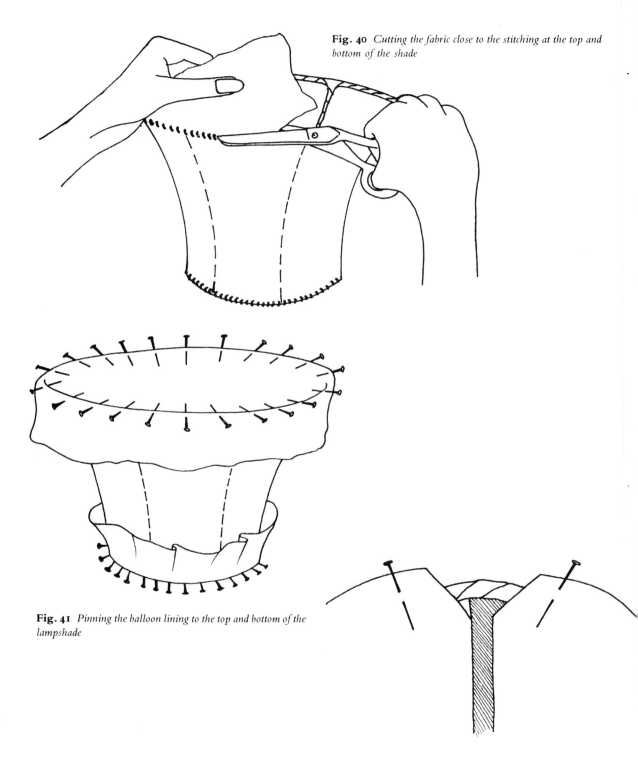

Fig. 40 *Cutting the fabric close to the stitching at the top and bottom of the shade*

Fig. 41 *Pinning the balloon lining to the top and bottom of the lampshade*

Fig. 42 *Spreading out the lining to fit round the gimbal fitting*

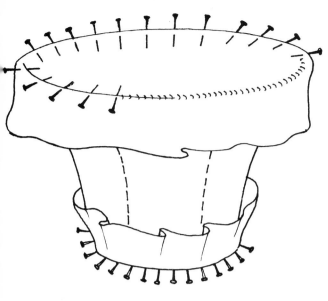

Fig. 43 *The balloon lining pinned and stitched into position*

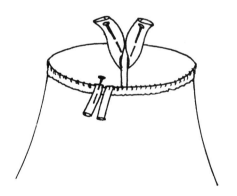

Figs 44 & 45 *Neatening the fitting*

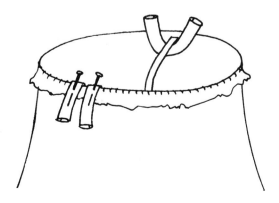

the outer edge of the top and bottom rings and should be worked from right to left (*fig. 39*).

(5) Cut away the surplus fabric from the top and bottom of the lampshade, trimming as close as possible to the stitches. If this fabric is not cut away very close to the stitching it will make a bulky finish when the lining is inserted (*fig. 40*).

Inserting the balloon lining

(1) Press the lining flat and do not press the seams open. Drop the lining into the shade matching the seams and horizontal pencil marks at the top and bottom rings. Make sure that there are no frayed edges, loose threads, or pins on the inside of the cover before the lining is inserted. If there are, they will show up and spoil the finished effect of the shade when it is lit.

(2) Pin the lining to the top and bottom rings, making sure that the pins are placed on the outer edge of the shade. Adjust the lining by tightening the pins at the top and bottom of the shade until the lining is taught and smooth and all fullness has been disposed of (*fig. 41*).

(3) When pinning the lining round the top ring, carefully unpick the seam down to the horizontal pencil mark and spread out the fabric to enable the lining to fit neatly round the gimbal fitting (*fig. 42*) or, if necessary, carefully cut the fabric in order to slip it around the fitting.

(4) Oversew the lining to the frame in the same way as for the outer cover, using short lengths of matching double thread (*fig. 43*). Position the stitches on the outer edge of the lampshade so that they are completely covered when the trimming is applied. Trim off close to the stitching.

Neatening the gimbal fitting

To neaten the fitting, cut a piece of lining fabric 10 cm (4 in) long by 2.5 cm (1 in) wide. Fold this into three to make a strip 1.3 cm ($\frac{1}{2}$ in) wide. Slip this under the fitting and pin into position as in figs 44 and 45. Oversew securely in place keeping the stitches well down on the stitching line on the outer edge of the shade.

On a large or standard shade the fitting is usually a duplex one and not a gimbal. Particular care must

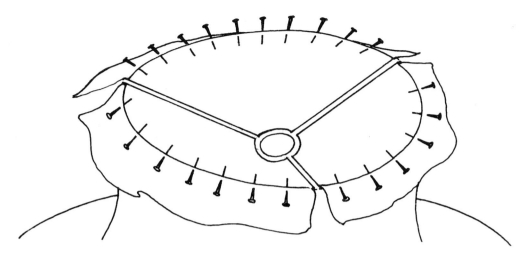

Fig. 46 *Lining slashed to fit round a duplex fitting*

be taken when applying the lining as it is necessary to slash down where the duplex fitting is fixed to the top ring in order to make the lining set well (*fig. 46*). Unless a deep enough cut is made the lining will pucker, but if too deep a cut is made an ugly gap will be visible in the lining. Care and accuracy are essential to achieve a neat fit round each wire of the fitting. This should then be neatened with a strip of fabric as described above.

Trimmings
Apply trimming to the top and bottom rings to cover the stitching according to the instructions given in Chapter 8.

Tiffany-style lampshades

Tiffany-style lampshades fit in well with both traditional and modern decorative schemes. They diffuse the light well because of their shape, and many different types of fabric can be used to make them. They are very versatile and look well when placed over dining room and kitchen tables; they add a touch of style to bathrooms and bedrooms and are useful in hallways and cloakrooms because of the amount of light they distribute. These lampshades can be made to match or co-ordinate with bed linen, table linen, curtains, wallpaper etc. and look effective made up in either cottons or silks.

There are two methods of covering this type of lampshade frame. The first, which is simple and quick, consists of making a tube with a casing at the top and bottom through which elastic is threaded. A lining is not often used, and the cover is easily removed for washing.

In the second method the fabric is cut and sewn to the frame in sections, which means that motifs and patterns can be positioned to advantage. Balloon linings are not practicable for this shape of frame, so a lining is sewn onto the frame first.

Tiffany-style frames vary considerably in shape, so buy one that is suitable for the method chosen.

Gathered tiffany lampshade with frill
This is only suitable for thin, lightweight fabrics that have good draping qualities, e.g. lace, lawn, voile and light dress cottons.

(1) Prepare and tape the top and bottom rings of the frame. It is not necessary to bind the struts but they should be painted to prevent rusting if they are not covered with a plastic coating.

(2) A rectangle of fabric is needed, which should be the length of the circumference of the bottom ring plus 10 cm (4 in). The width should be the measurement of the strut plus 7.5 cm (3 in). If it is necessary to join the fabric to obtain the required length, cut two pieces of equal size. Join with a French seam to make a tube. Press seam flat.

Fig. 47 *Tiffany-style lampshades*

(3) Make a casing at the top and bottom edge. Turn over 1.3 cm ($\frac{1}{2}$ in) and press; then turn over another 1.3 cm ($\frac{1}{2}$ in) and press. Machine along the top and bottom edges of the casing leaving 1.3 cm ($\frac{1}{2}$ in) open for inserting the elastic (*fig. 48*).

(4) Thread a narrow tape or a piece of string through the casing at the top and bottom and place on to the frame. Adjust to fit and mark the tape to get the length of elastic required.

(5) Mark the position of the frill with tailors' chalk or tacking thread. This is the fitting line (*fig. 49*). Take the cover off the shade and insert the requisite

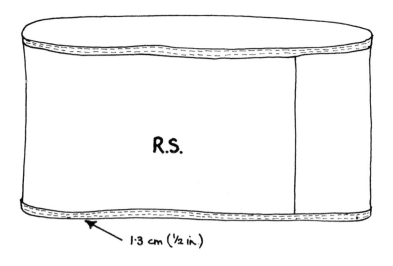

R.S.

1·3 cm (½ in.)

Fig. 48 *Casing machine stitched, leaving 1.3 cm ($\frac{1}{2}$ in) for elastic*

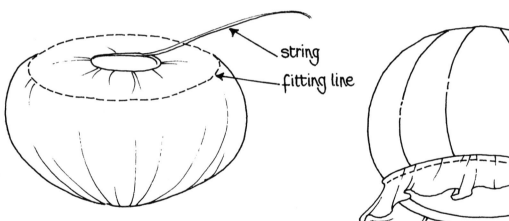

string

fitting line

Fig. 49 *Adjusting the cover to fit the frame and marking the fitting line with a tacking thread*

Fig. 51 *The frill tacked into position on the lampshade*

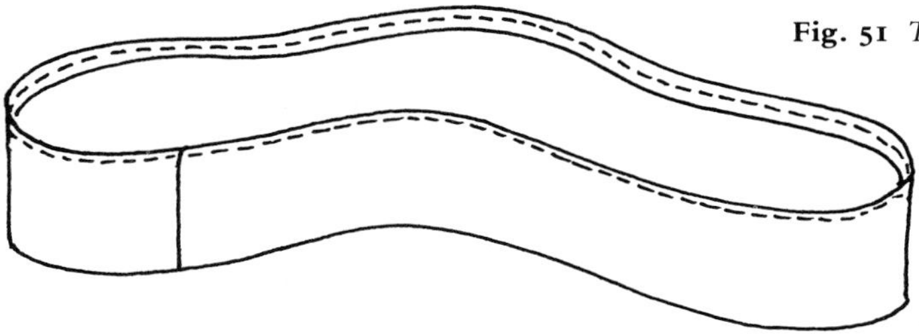

Fig. 50 *Running stitch for frill passes through two layers of fabric*

length of elastic, sewing the ends firmly together.

(6) To make a frill, cut a strip of fabric on the straight grain 10–15 cm (4–6 in) wide and one and a half to twice the circumference of the bottom ring (depending on the thickness of the fabric). Join the ends of the strip with a narrow French seam. Fold in half lengthwise and turn in raw edges 1.3 cm ($\frac{1}{2}$ in) at the top edge. Make a row of running stitches along the fabric 10 mm ($\frac{3}{8}$ in) from the top edge (*fig. 50*). Gather up the frill and adjust to fit the bottom of the lampshade. Apply the frill to the shade along the fitting line (*fig. 51*).

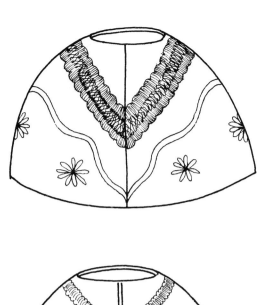

Tailored tiffany lampshade

Many different fabrics can be used for this style of shade as the material is stretched onto the frame on the cross of the grain in four separate sections. Suitable fabrics include silks, satins, light furnishing cottons, polyester/cotton sheeting and broderie anglaise. Also suitable are pieces of lace and embroidery as well as fabric that has been painted and dyed, such as batik work or tie-and-dyed material. Fabrics with dominant motifs or designs can be positioned effectively, but pronounced, even stripes and checks should be avoided as they are often difficult to match successfully. However, some patterns and striped fabrics can look very effective if positioned carefully (*figs 52–54*) and make delightful shades. With this method, do not use a frame that has a very marked convex curve at the top and bottom (see fig. 15), for this type usually has too many struts and is more successful when made up in the gathered style.

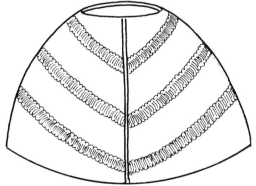

(1) Prepare and tape the frame. When a plastic-coated frame is used and the lining fabric chosen is white, it is only necessary to bind the top and bottom rings and the struts on to which pinning and sewing will take place (*fig. 55*). However, if a coloured lining is being used it is best to bind all the struts and then dye the tape to the shade of the lining fabric. As the struts will show on the finished lampshade, this gives a more pleasing and uniform appearance.

(2) To obtain an accurate estimate of the amount of fabric needed, measure the size of one quarter of the frame and make a rough paper pattern. Allow generous turnings all round (approximately 7.5 cm

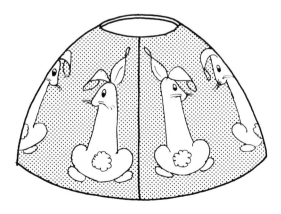

Figs 52, 53 & **54** *Patterns positioned effectively on tiffany-style lampshades*

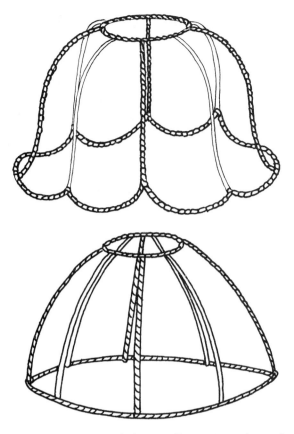

Fig. 55 *In some cases only the top and bottom rings and some of the struts need to be bound with tape*

helpful to use a curved needle for sewing over some parts of the curves.)

(4) Trim fabric away from the two struts close to the stitching, but at the top and bottom rings (AB and CD) trim it so as to leave 5 cm (2 in) for neatening the edges when the top cover has been applied (*fig. 60*). Fit and sew the lining to the other three quarters of the frame in the same way.

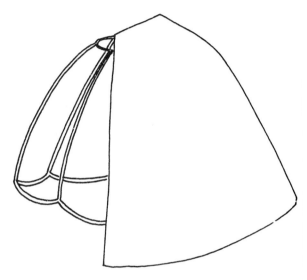

Fig. 56 *Making a paper pattern in order to estimate the amount of fabric needed for a tailored tiffany lampshade*

[3 in]). Four pieces of fabric approximately this size will be required, and must be cut on the cross grain of the fabric (*figs 56 and 57*). If motifs or patterns need to be centralized or matched, a little more fabric must, of course, be allowed. Approximately $\frac{1}{2}$–$\frac{3}{4}$ metre (yard) of both cover and lining fabric is usually sufficient for an average-sized frame where plain or random match patterned fabric is used.

(3) Fit the lining fabric over a quarter of the frame on the cross of the grain, placing pins at A B C and D to hold the fabric to the frame. Pin to the top and bottom rings AB and CD and down the two struts AC and BD, gently easing out the fullness (*fig. 58*). When all the fullness has been disposed of and the fabric is smooth and taut, oversew the fabric to the frame using matching double thread. Work from B to A then CD and back to B (*fig. 59*). (It can be

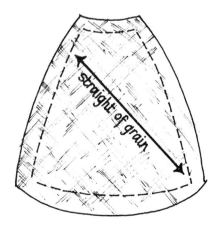

Fig. 57 *Paper pattern for a tailored tiffany lampshade allows generous turning allowances*

(5) When the lining is complete apply the top cover in the same way, using the same struts for fitting and stitching each quarter section. Trim the cover fabric at the top and bottom rings close to the stitching (*fig. 61*).

(6) Neaten the top and bottom rings by folding the lining fabric over the top cover and stitch with a single thread using one small and one long stitch

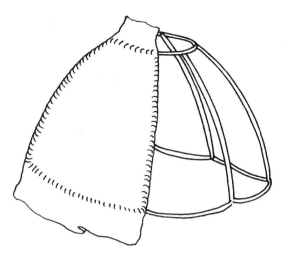

Fig. 60 *The lining trimmed close to the stitching on the struts leaving approximately 5 cm (2 in) at the top and bottom rings for neatening the edges*

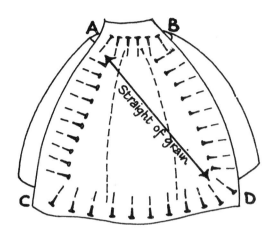

Fig. 58 *Lining fabric pinned to the frame. Note the position of the pins*

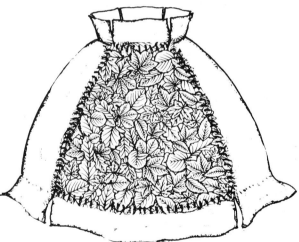

Fig. 61 *Cover fabric trimmed away close to stitching*

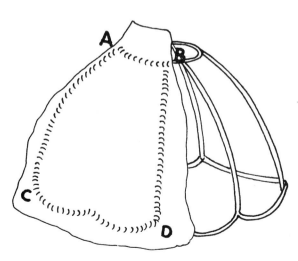

Fig. 59 *Lining fabric sewn into position over one quarter of the frame*

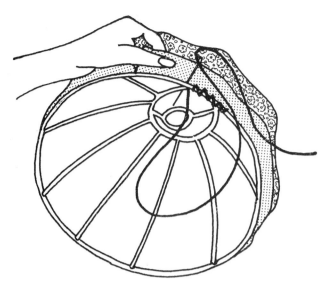

Fig. 62 *Neatening the bottom ring by folding the lining fabric over the top cover and stitching into position*

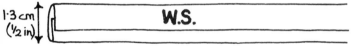

1·3 cm (½ in)

W.S.

Fig. 63 *Crossway strip folded to make a trimming*

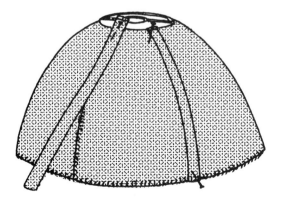

Fig. 64 *Neatening the stitches on the struts with crossway strips*

(*fig. 62*). Keep the stitches well over to the front of the lampshade so that they will be covered by the trimming. Trim off close to the stitching.

(7) To neaten the stitches on the struts prepare four crossway strips 3.2 cm (1¼ in) wide, the length of the strut plus 2.5 cm (1 in) (see instructions on page 81). Fold into three to make a strip approximately 1.3 cm (½ in) wide (*fig. 63*).

(8) Apply adhesive to the wrong side (W.S.) of one end of the strip and secure it to the top ring. Place a pin at the top ring to hold the strip firmly in position whilst the rest of the strip is applied. Stretch the strip slightly and position over the stitching on the strut. Press it firmly to the shade with the fingers, making sure it adheres firmly to the shade. Apply the strip two or three centimetres (inches) at a time so that a perfectly even finish is achieved. Put a pin at the bottom ring to hold the strip firmly until the adhesive has dried thoroughly (*fig. 64*).

This is an important process in the finishing of the lampshade, and care and patience are needed. Use a small fruit or kitchen knife to apply the adhesive to

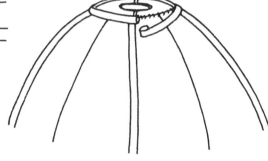

Fig. 65 *Applying the crossway strip to the top of a lampshade*

the strip, spreading it evenly and carefully a little at a time. Take care that the adhesive does not mark the fabric; if too much is used on fine fabrics it will soak through and mark the right side of the strip, and this is difficult to remove successfully.

(9) The top and bottom rings can be trimmed with a suitable braid or fringe (see page 73), or can be finished with a crossway strip. When attaching this strip to the top and bottom of a shade apply the end of it to the outside edge of the shade, starting 6 mm

($\frac{1}{4}$ in) beyond a strut. The strip should just cover the oversewing stitches but should not extend to the inside of the shade. To finish off, turn in 6 mm ($\frac{1}{4}$ in) at the end of the strip, secure with a little adhesive, and apply over the starting end (*fig. 65*).

Pleated lampshades

These can be made using either swathed pleating or straight or diagonal pleats, or a combination of both. Attractive effects can also be obtained with 'sunray' and 'fan' pleating. A certain amount of care and patience is needed when making these more advanced lampshades if a professional result is to be achieved, but they are certainly most rewarding and well worth the time and effort involved. Their success lies in accurate pleating and attractive colour combinations. There is great scope for imagination and originality when planning these shades and some ideas are shown in figs 66–76.

Choose soft sheer fabrics with good draping qualities such as silk or rayon chiffon, jap silk or silk shantung. Nylon and some man-made fabrics are not suitable as they do not always pleat well and are very springy, which makes them difficult to handle. Silk shantung can be used for straight pleating but chiffon is preferable for swathed styles.

Although these fabrics give the best results when making the traditional style of pleated or swathed lampshades, polyester/cotton sheeting and some light furnishing cottons can also be used effectively. These are best made in the recently popular coolie

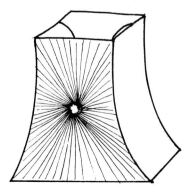

Fig. 66 *One section of a lampshade worked in sun-ray pleating*

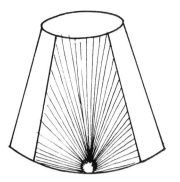

Fig. 67 *Straight-sided empire frame worked in sun-ray pleating*

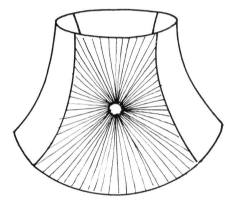

Fig. 68 *Sun-ray pleating with a central motif worked on a bowed empire frame*

Fig. 69 *Straight-pleated lampshade with collar*

Fig. 70 *Bedlight with sun-ray pleating*

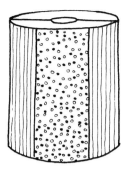

Fig. 71 *Drum lampshade with pleated sections*

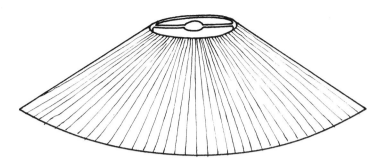

Fig. 72 *Coolie-style pleated lampshade*

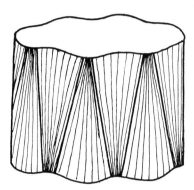

Fig. 73 *Fan pleating used on a fluted drum lampshade*

Fig. 74 *Pleated drum lampshade*

Fig. 75 *Swathed pleating on a bowed empire lampshade*

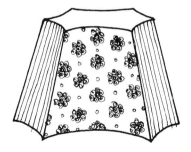

Fig. 76 *Panelled shade with pleated ends*

and drum shapes if a co-ordinating furnishing scheme is planned.

When making pleated shades an external lining is fitted and sewn to the shade before the cover is pleated. This gives a firm foundation on which to work and prevents any movement of the pleats once they have been worked. However, with some more intricate shades it is necessary to have an interlining as well as a lining, as for example with the sun-ray pleated styles (see pages 49–51).

Pleated drum lampshade

(**1**) Choose a frame that has straight, not curved sides or struts.

(2) To estimate the amount of fabric needed for the pleating allow $2\frac{1}{2}$–3 times the circumference of the bottom ring and the depth of the frame plus 5 cm (2 in).

(3) Bind the frame and prepare and make the lining as on page 31. An external lining is used on this type of shade instead of a balloon lining so that the pleating is not disturbed once it has been worked.

(4) Fit the lining over the top of the lampshade frame on the outside of the struts and pin as in fig. 77. At the bottom ring make a slash at each strut, fold in the lining 3 mm ($\frac{1}{8}$ in) and pin over onto the front of the bottom ring as in fig. 77. The lining at the top of the shade is simply pinned and sewn on to the outside of the top ring; no slashing down to the struts is necessary here. Oversew the lining to the top and bottom rings in the usual way.

(5) Trim the lining to the stitching at the bottom ring, but at the top ring trim off to leave 2.5 cm (1 in) for neatening the edge when the pleating has been worked.

Working the pleats

(1) Tear or cut the fabric into strips the depth required. (Chiffon is best torn to get a smooth straight edge.) The pleating should run down the selvedge grain of the fabric. This is important as there is a definite grain to chiffon and some other fabrics, and the pleats will set well if the material is used in this way. The strips of fabric are not seamed together but are folded over one another during pleating.

(2) Decide on the width of the pleat and whether or not a space is required between each. Pleats can vary in width from 6 mm–1.3 cm ($\frac{1}{4}$–$\frac{1}{2}$ in), the choice being governed to some extent by the thickness of the fabric used, smaller pleats being more appropriate on finer fabrics.

(3) Turn in the raw edge of the fabric the width of one pleat and pin in position at the top and bottom rings over a side strut. Leave 1.3 cm ($\frac{1}{2}$ in) of fabric extending beyond the bottom ring and make sure that the grain of the fabric is in line with the fold of the pleat (*fig. 78*). Pleat and pin the fabric along the bottom ring until the next strut is reached, making sure that the 1.3 cm ($\frac{1}{2}$ in) overlap at the bottom ring

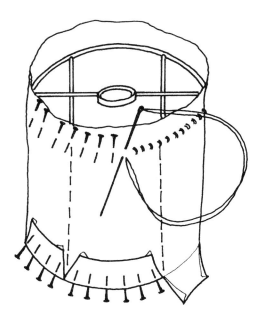

Fig. 77 *Lining pinned to frame with slashes made at struts on the bottom ring*

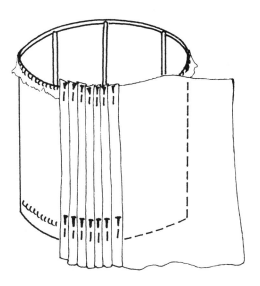

Fig. 78 *Pleating pinned into position at the top and bottom rings*

45

is kept perfectly straight and that the fold lines of each pleat are in line with the grain of the fabric. This is the secret of successful pleating. If it is not done accurate pleating will not be achieved.

(4) At the end of one section of the frame complete the pleating by drawing up the fabric to the top ring and pin it into position (*fig. 78*). Oversew the pleating in the usual way at the top and bottom ring, using double matching thread. Leave the first pleat pinned and do not stitch down. Make quite sure that each pleat is taut and that it is stitched securely.

(5) Continue pleating, carefully pinning and sewing one section at a time until the last strut is reached. Make sure that the same number of pleats is worked into each section. Finish off the pleating by slipping the end of the last pleat underneath the first one (which has not been stitched down – see 4 above) and complete the stitching. When joining the strips of fabric, simply overlap the fabric at the end of the first set of pleating to form another pleat. If possible, try to have this join on a strut even if it means trimming away a little surplus fabric. Take care to cut the fabric with a sharp pair of scissors to obtain a smooth edge.

(6) To neaten the lining at the top ring trim the fabric back to the stitching and fold the lining over the pleating. Stitch as in fig. 79, using one large and one small oversewing stitch and a single thread. Neaten the bottom edge by folding the fabric back and sewing in the same way. Trim off to the stitching.

(7) Attach the trimming round the top and bottom rings as explained on page 74.

This method can also be used for straight-sided empire and cone shapes, but when using these it is advisable to have a space between each pleat on the bottom ring to allow for the overlap of the pleating at the smaller top ring. The same number of pleats have to be fitted into a smaller space, so the size of the space at the bottom ring must be adjusted to suit the individual lampshade.

When making a pleated lampshade with a collar, the pleating should be stitched to the lower ring of the collar before being drawn up and pleated to the top ring (*fig. 80*).

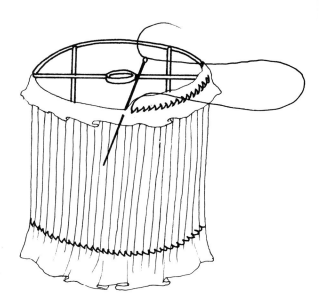

Fig. 79 *Neatening the lining by folding over the pleating*

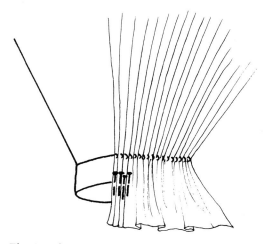

Fig. 80 *Pleating is stitched into place on the lower ring of the collar before being pleated and sewn to the top ring*

Fan-pleated lampshade

This style of shade is worked in the same way as a straight pleated shade and follows the same basic principles. Care must be taken, however, to measure and mark out the arrangement for each set of pleats on the top and bottom rings before the work is started. Use a straight-sided or fluted drum frame for this type of pleating (*figs 73 and 74*).

Small sets of pleats should be made alternately at the top and bottom rings, and then drawn up and stitched in the usual way. A separate piece of fabric must be used for each set of pleats, and is very effective if worked in two colours of chiffon, or in two tones of one colour (*figs 81 and 82*). The size of each set of pleats is governed by the design and size of the frame.

Swathed pleated lampshade

To be successful these lampshades require a little more skill than the straight pleated styles, so if possible make a straight pleated one first to gain experience and confidence with the pleating.

Pure silk chiffons and georgettes give the best results as they are easier to handle than man-made fabrics and do not fray. As these fabrics are rather fine, the finished effect of the lampshade is enhanced by the insertion of an interlining as well as a balloon lining. This gives body to the pleating, particularly where a dark-coloured fabric is being used over a light-coloured lining. In this case use the same fabric for the interlining as for the pleating. A more pleasing effect is obtained when the bulb is lit.

(1) Use a curved empire frame in either an oval or a round style. A straight-sided empire or a drum is not suitable as the effect of the swathing would be lost on this shape of frame.

(2) Prepare and bind the frame (see page 27).

(3) To estimate the amount of fabric needed for the pleating measure the circumference of the bottom ring and multiply by three to obtain the width. To obtain the depth measure the lampshade with a tape measure from the bottom of the first strut A and up and across to the top ring B, missing out one strut (*fig. 83*). Add 5 cm (2 in) to this measurement.

(4) Prepare and make the balloon lining as for the classic lampshade (page 31), using crepe-backed satin or a similar fabric, and set aside.

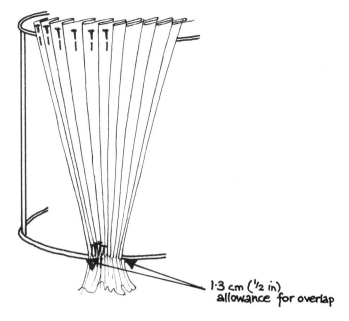

Fig. 81 *First set of fan pleating pinned into position showing an allowance of 1.3 cm (½ in) at each side of the pleating*

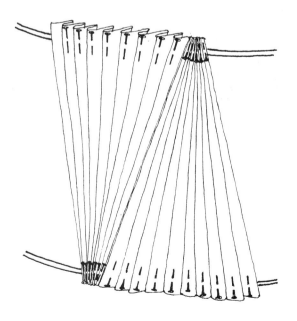

Fig. 82 *Second set of fan pleating pinned into position*

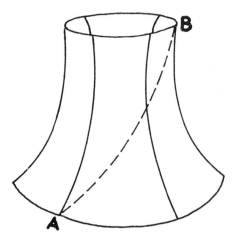

Fig. 83 *Measuring for a swathed pleated lampshade*

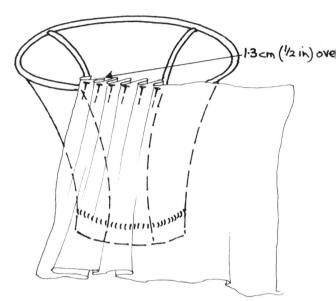

Fig. 85 *Pleating along the bottom ring showing a 1.3 cm ($\frac{1}{2}$ in) overlap*

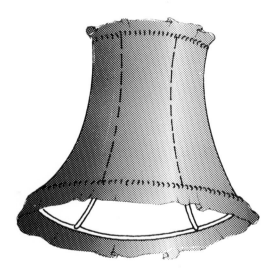

Fig. 84 *Interlining for a swathed shade made in chiffon to match the pleated cover*

(5) Prepare and apply the interlining. This is made as for the cover for the classic shade (page 31) and is best made in chiffon or georgette to match the pleating (*fig. 84*).

(6) Prepare the chiffon or georgette for the pleating by tearing or cutting it into strips of the required depth. Cut off the selvedges. Ideally, georgette should not be ironed before use because this removes the crinkled effect from the fabric. If necessary, however, press lightly with a warm iron to remove any creases.

(7) Pin the first pleat into position, folding in the raw edge. Make the pleats from 6–10 mm ($\frac{1}{4}$–$\frac{3}{8}$ in) wide. Pleat and pin the fabric on to the bottom ring until one section of the frame has been completed (*fig. 85*). Leave an equal space between each pleat and take care to keep the fold of the pleat in line with the grain of the fabric, keeping a 1.3 cm ($\frac{1}{2}$ in) overlap along the bottom ring (*fig. 85*).

(8) To swathe the fabric to the top ring, take the first pleat and drape it up and across to the top ring, stretching the fabric gently. Miss the next strut and pin to the following one (*fig. 86*). Drape each pleat in turn. There must be the same number of pleats at the top ring as at the bottom ring, but as the same amount of fabric has to be fitted into the top section, the pleats there will of necessity be much smaller and will be much closer and may overlap (*fig. 87*).

1 Pleated 'coolie' lampshade made in light furnishing cotton

2 *Petal shaped shade on a Chinese base*

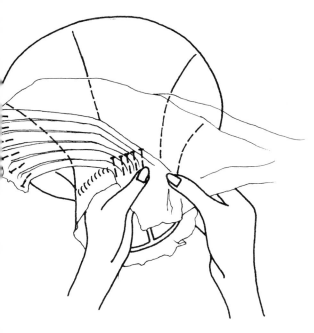

Fig. 86 *Swathing the pleating to the top ring missing out one strut*

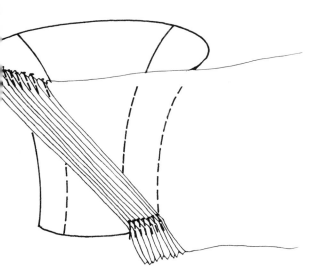

Fig. 87 *Pleating pinned into position on one section showing overlap of pleats at the top ring*

(9) When one section has been pleated satisfactorily, adjust the pins at both the top and bottom rings making sure that the pleats are taut and flat.

(10) Oversew this section at the top and bottom rings, leaving the first pleat pinned, so that the last pleat can be tucked underneath at the completion of the pleating.

(11) Continue pleating and draping each section in turn, checking carefully that each has the same number of pleats.

(12) At the last strut cut off the material with a sharp pair of scissors to achieve a smooth straight edge and tuck underneath the first pleat. Complete the stitching.

(13) Trim off the chiffon at the top and bottom rings of both the interlining and the pleating fabric. Insert the prepared balloon lining as on page 35 (classic shade) taking care to disturb the pleats as little as possible when sewing.

(14) Apply the trimming. Metallic laces and narrow velvet ribbons look particularly effective on pleated and swathed lampshades. The lace should be sewn on in the usual way and the velvet ribbon is best applied with an adhesive (see page 74). A trimming made from a strip of chiffon or georgette can also be used successfully. If this is chosen tear off a long strip 1.3–1.9 cm ($\frac{1}{2}$–$\frac{3}{4}$ in) wide along the selvedge before the strips are prepared for pleating. This obviates the need for joins in the trimming.

Sun-ray pleated lampshade
Several styles of frame are suitable for this type of pleating, as only one or two of the sections or panels are pleated. Frames with concave panels should be avoided, however, as their shape would be altered by this method of pleating. Sun-ray pleated shades require a firm interlining to support the pleating, as well as a lining.

(1) Prepare and bind the frame.

(2) To estimate the amount of fabric required for the pleated panel, measure round the section of the frame to be pleated and allow twice that measurement to obtain the width. Measure from the position of the motif to the bottom ring at its widest point (AB) and add 5 cm (2 in) to obtain the depth (*fig. 88*).

(3) Prepare an interlining and a lining for the frame following the instructions for the classic shade on page 31. These are best made in crepe-backed satin or similar fabric.

(4) Apply and sew the interlining firmly into position on the frame. This is particularly important as it provides the foundation for the sun-ray pleating.

(5) Measure and mark out the section to be pleated into four equal parts and mark the position for the motif (*fig. 88*).

(6) Cut or tear the pleating fabric into strips of the required depth and width. Make two rows of gathering stitches along one of the long sides 6 mm (¼ in) from the raw edge. If necessary, join the strips together with the gathering stitches. With tailor tacks mark off the strip of fabric into four equal sections (*fig. 89*). Draw up the gathering threads tightly into a small circle and sew firmly to the interlining at the centre of the section (*fig. 90*).

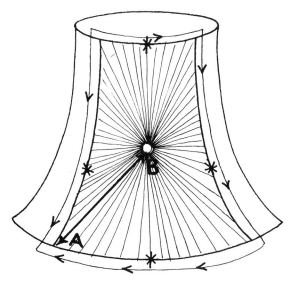

Fig. 88 *Measuring and estimating fabric requirements for a sun-ray pleated panel. Note that the section is marked into four equal parts*

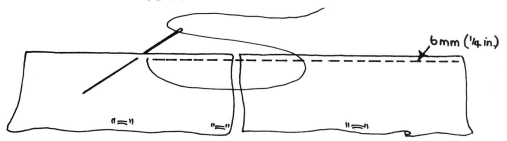

Fig. 89 *Strip of fabric marked into four equal sections with tailor tacks*

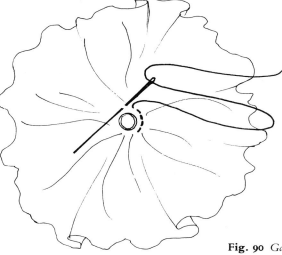

Fig. 90 *Gathering threads drawn up and sewn to the centre of the section*

(7) Pin the outer edges of the circle of fabric to the frame, matching guide marks and tailor tacks (*fig. 91*). Space the pleats evenly round the section. Oversew into position and trim off the fabric to the stitching. Apply the motif firmly to the gathered raw edge in the centre (*fig. 92*). A motif could be made by covering a button to match the pleating. Alternatively, a motif of hand-made lace or Guipure lace could be used.

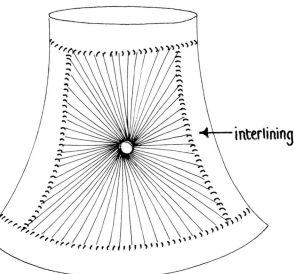

Fig. 92 *Central motif applied over raw edges of pleated fabric*

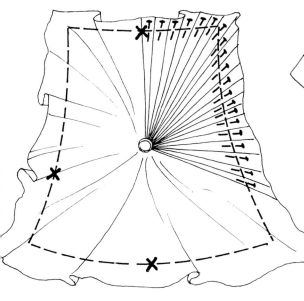

Fig. 91 *Pinning the pleating to the frame at the outer edges of the circle of fabric*

(8) Insert the balloon lining as on page 35.

(9) Apply crossway strip or a narrow braid to neaten the stitches on the struts and apply a suitable trimming to the top and bottom rings of the lampshade (see Chapter 8).

Pleated coolie lampshade
The method described on page 45 is also suitable for coolie shapes, or the following method can be used. Here, the fabric at the lower ring is gathered instead of pleated and is drawn up to the top ring in pleats (*fig. 93*).

Fig. 93 *Outer cover gathered at the bottom ring and pleated at the top ring*

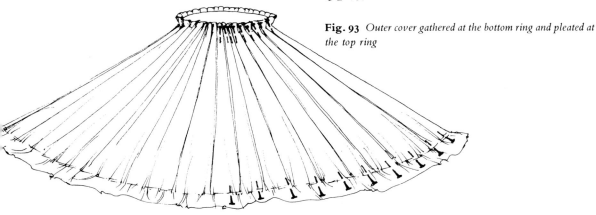

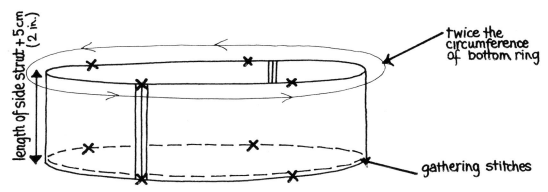

length of side strut + 5 cm (2 in.)

twice the circumference of bottom ring

gathering stitches

Fig. 94 *Preparing the fabric for a coolie shade showing the fabric marked into four equal sections*

Light cottons, polyester/cotton sheeting and silk shantungs are suitable fabrics for this style of shade, as well as silk and rayon chiffons.

To estimate the amount of fabric needed allow $2-2\frac{1}{2}$ times the circumference of the bottom ring and the length of the side strut plus 5 cm (2 in). Choose a frame that has straight, not curved struts.

(1) Prepare and bind the frame. As the struts will show on the finished shade it is best to dye the tape to the shade of the lining fabric. This can be done with a cold water dye when the frame has been bound.

(2) Make and fit the lining as for the pleated drum lampshade (see page 44).

(3) Join the strips of fabric for the outer cover to make a tube measuring approximately twice the circumference of the bottom of the shade, by the length of one of the side struts plus 5 cm (2 in). Make joins with flat seams, and press open. Work two rows of gathering stitches along one of the long sides of the fabric 6 mm ($\frac{1}{4}$ in) from the raw edge. Divide the fabric into quarters, and mark with tailor's tacks or pins (*fig. 94*). Mark the lampshade into quarters on the bottom and top rings so that each section of the outer cover can be fitted to a corresponding section of the lampshade frame.

(4) Place the outer cover on to the frame over the lining and pin the guide marks to the corresponding ones on the frame. Draw up the gathering threads to make the fabric fit the bottom ring, adjusting the gathers evenly. Pin and oversew into position using double matching thread.

(5) Draw the fabric up to make small pleats at the top ring. Check that the pleats are even in size and that each section fits into the corresponding section on the frame. Pin and oversew into position (*fig. 93*).

(6) Trim off the fabric to the stitching and neaten the top and bottom rings by folding the lining over the pleating. Stitch as in fig. 79, using one large and one small oversewing stitch and a single thread. Trim off to the stitching.

(7) Apply trimming to the top and bottom of the lampshade.

Coolie lampshade with pleated lining

When a tailored cover is made for a coolie lampshade a pleated lining can make an attractive finish. This type of lining is also effective when used on a fluted drum shape where the lining is easily visible, and on some shapes of lampshade frames with collars.

(1) Prepare and bind the frame.

(2) Prepare and fit the cover to the lampshade frame, trimming the fabric close to the stitching at the top and bottom rings.

(3) To cut the strip of fabric needed for the lining measure round the bottom ring and add 1.3 cm ($\frac{1}{2}$ in) for turnings. This measurement must be taken accurately as the lining must be exactly the right size. If it is too tight it will not fit over the frame and

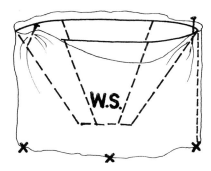

Fig. 95 *Pinning the lining into position on the lower ring*

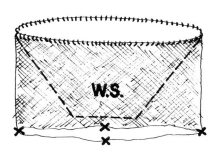

Fig. 96 *The lining stitched into position on the lower ring*

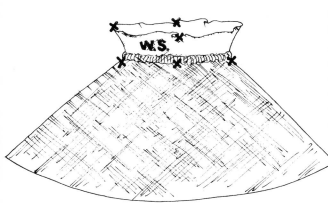

Fig. 97 *The lining drawn up inside the lampshade to the top ring ready for pleating*

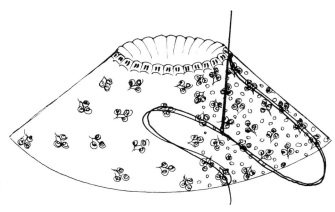

Fig. 98 *Sewing the pleating into position at the top ring*

if it is too big the lining will be loose and baggy round the bottom ring. The width of the strip must be the length of one of the side struts plus 3.8 cm ($1\frac{1}{2}$ in).

(4) Join the strip with a flat seam to make a tube that fits exactly round the bottom ring of the frame. Divide into four equal sections and mark with tailor tacks. Mark the lampshade into quarters on the top ring.

(5) Slip the lining over the cover of the lampshade and pin into position round the bottom ring with the wrong sides facing (*fig. 95*). Position the seam at a side strut.

(6) Oversew with double matching thread making sure that the stitches are worked on the bottom edge of the ring (*fig. 96*).

(7) Draw the lining up inside the frame and pull over on to the outside of the top ring. Pin into small even pleats fitting each marked section into the corresponding quarter of the top ring (*fig. 97*). Slash fabric where necessary to fit round the gimbal or other fitting.

(8) Oversew with double matching thread on the outer edge of the ring (*fig. 98*) and trim off close to the stitching.

(9) Apply trimming to the top and bottom of the lampshade.

Fig. 99 *Petal-shaped lampshades*

Fig. 100 *Bed-head frames*

54

Square and sectional lampshades

This method of making lampshades is the best one to use for square and sectional lampshades or for unusual shapes such as the petal-shaped frames in fig. 99. It is a useful method for three-quarter shades and shields, such as bedhead lights or when using fabric that has little stretch or elasticity (*fig. 100*). It is particularly useful when using fabrics that would not normally be considered suitable for lampshades, such as glazed chintz, velvets and embroidered panels. Pieces of fine sewing, for example, pulled thread work, quilting, and bobbin laces, can be accurately centred on the frame when worked in this way.

Each panel or section is sewn to the frame separately or sometimes two or three panels can be worked together. Either an external or balloon lining is used, depending on the shape of the frame. With some pieces of fine sewing an interlining would enhance the finished shade. Where possible, prepare and make the lining as in (2) and (3) below, but for unusual shapes or for 30.5 cm (12 in) or larger square or rectangular frames, apply the lining in sections in the same way as for the outer cover, as this prevents the lining from puckering when the cover is applied.

Square or oblong shape

(1) Prepare and bind the frame.

(2) Prepare and make an external lining stretching the fabric over half of the frame with the right sides together (*fig. 101*). Because of its shape it is difficult to fit a balloon lining to this style of shade.

(3) Fit the lining over the outside of the frame making sure that the seams are positioned on two of the side struts with the raw edges on the outside of the frame. Pin and oversew to the frame using matching double thread (*fig. 102*).

(4) For the top cover work the two larger sections first and then the two smaller side ones. With the fabric on the cross grain, place the material over the front section of the frame. Pin at the top and bottom of the frame using only a few pins to hold the fabric in position (*fig. 103*).

(5) Insert three pins halfway down the section at

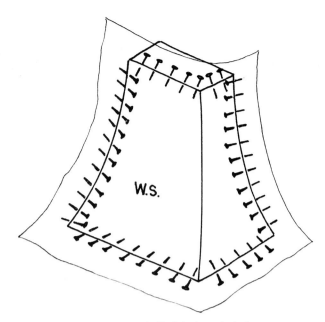

Fig. 101 *Lining pinned to half of the lampshade frame*

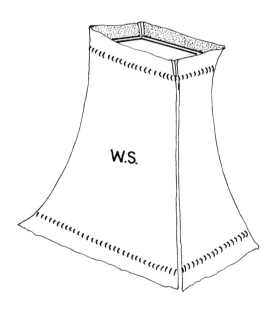

Fig. 102 *Lining stitched into position, having the two seams on the struts*

55

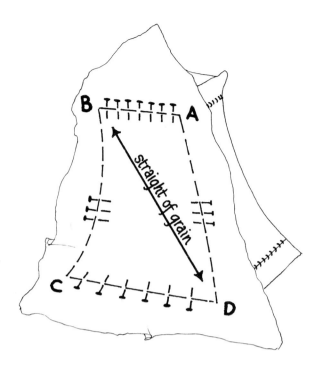

Fig. 103 *Pinning a sectional lampshade with the straight grain of the fabric placed diagonally on the frame*

both sides, pulling gently across the frame. Continue pinning down both sides and along the top and bottom of the frame, stretching the fabric gently to mould to the shape of the frame.

(6) After pinning all four sides work round the section removing each pin in turn, making sure that the fabric is firm and taut and free from wrinkles or creases.

(7) When the panel has been satisfactorily pinned and stretched, oversew with double matching thread starting at the top right hand corner A (*fig. 103*). Work along the top of the frame to B, down to the bottom ring CD and up to A.

(8) Work the back section in the same way and then the two side sections.

(9) Trim away the cover fabric to the stitching and neaten the edges by folding over the lining to the front of the lampshade. Finish as in fig. 79.

(10) Neaten each corner strut with a crossway strip in matching fabric (see page 81) and apply a trimming to the top and bottom of the lampshade.

Wall lights and candle shades

These small shades are constructed in the same way as full-size ones, but because they are so much smaller they are often more awkward to handle. However, as they are costly to buy they are well worth the effort involved.

Shades for wall lights and chandelier-type fittings are usually fixed with a butterfly clip which enables the shade to clip on to the bulb. These clips vary in size and can be especially small to fit on to candle-size bulbs or larger to fit on to standard bulbs (*figs 105 and 106*). Before buying the lampshade frames check the light fitting to see which type of clip is required.

Balloon linings would become scorched and discoloured in a short time if used on such small shades, so use an external lining. The use of low wattage bulbs also minimizes the risk of discoloration and scorching.

Frames for wall lights and central chandelier-type fittings come in a limited range of basic shapes, but sometimes unusual designs can be found. Alternatively, old frames can be recovered provided they are in good shape and are carefully stripped and prepared (see page 27).

Half shades and shields are suitable for use where only the front of the shade is visible. Three-quarter shades are the best choice for situations where the shade is viewed from the side as well. These give a more pleasing effect as they cover more of the bulb than a half shade.

The light from half and three-quarter shades is reflected against the wall and back into the room, so they give more light than a full shade. They are not, of course, suitable for chandelier-type light fittings as they do not hide the bulb completely. Choose light-coloured linings with shiny surfaces to reflect the maximum amount of light.

When making half and three-quarter shades follow the instructions for making sectional shades on page 55. The trimming on these shades must be applied all round the frame in order to cover the stitching. Take care to mitre the corners of the trimming carefully and make sure that the join in the trim is placed in the most inconspicuous position possible (usually at the side of the shade at its lower edge) (*fig. 107*).

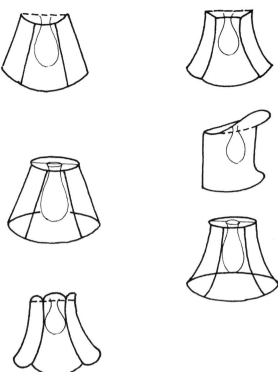

Fig. 104 *Some frames suitable for wall brackets and candelabra-type lights*

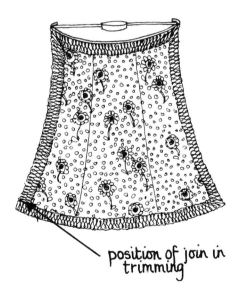

Fig. 106 *Large butterfly clip for larger bulbs*

position of join in trimming

Fig. 107 *Applying a trimming to a half shade showing the position of the join*

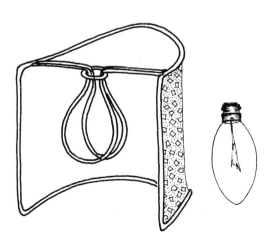

Fig. 105 *Small butterfly clip and candle bulb*

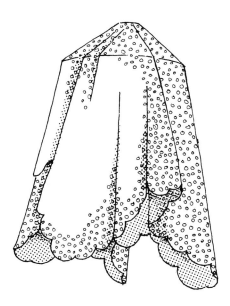

Fig. 108 *Handkerchief-style lampshade*

Fig. 109 *Mushroom coolie frame*

Fig. 110 *Using a square piece of fabric to make a handkerchief-style shade*

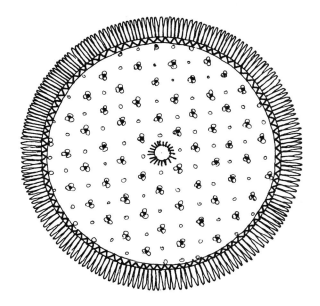

Fig. 111 *Using a circular piece of fabric to make a handkerchief-style shade*

When making full shades for wall lights or candelabra-type fittings follow the instructions for the classic shade on page 31. The lining is prepared in the same way but is applied to the frame before the top cover (*fig. 84*). The cover is then placed over the top of the lining and stitched in the usual way. To neaten the top and bottom rings, trim off the cover fabric to the stitching and fold the lining over the top cover and stitch as in fig. 79. Use one large and one small oversewing stitch and a single thread. Trim off to the stitching. Apply a trimming round the top and bottom rings taking care to choose one that both matches the size of the lampshade and covers the stitching adequately.

Handkerchief-style lampshades

This simple style of lampshade can be made very easily by draping a circular or square piece of fabric over a mushroom coolie frame. Alternatively, use a lampshade ring with a pendant or gimbal fitting (*figs 108 and 109*). For best effect the fabric should drop at least 30.5 cm (12 in) over the side of the frame. The edge can be finished in several ways.

(1) Cut a square piece of fabric to the size required and find the centre by folding it in four.

(2) Snip a hole at the centre point. Make sure that this is at least 2.5 cm (1 in) in diameter (or large enough to allow the electric flex to be threaded through easily). Buttonhole stitch round the raw edge (*fig. 110*).

(3) Finish the outer edges with a lampshade trimming or lace edge (*fig. 111*). Alternatively, the edges can be hemstitched or scalloped using machine embroidery or hand stitching. (When making a decorative hem or edge allow 2.5 cm [1 in] for turnings.) Slip the fabric over the lampshade frame or ring and thread the electric flex through the centre hole.

SEVEN
Firm lampshades

Firm or rigid lampshades are quick and easy to make, and very attractive shades can be achieved with a little imagination and the minimum of effort. Their crisp, uncluttered lines make them an ideal choice to complement the furnishings of today.

Interesting results can be obtained by combining or decorating these lampshades with other crafts and skills, for example, appliqué, patchwork, fabric printing, batik. Dried flowers, leaves and grasses can also be used effectively, but should be covered with acetate film for protection.

Keep trimmings on firm lampshades simple, matching them in weight and texture to the fabric of the shade. Some commercially made trimmings, although suitable for soft shades, are quite unsuitable for the firm shades. For example, if using hessian for the cover fabric choose a trimming to complement its rough texture. Plaited rushes, coarse wool or a cotton trimming would be a good choice. Thick piping cord can be used effectively on some firm shades and can, if necessary, be dyed to match the cover fabric.

Firm lampshades can be made with strutted frames or with a ring set. This consists of two rings, one with a fitting and the other one plain (*fig. 112*).

Choose the correct fitting for the type of shade and a suitably firm fabric for covering. This forms the shape of the shade (*fig. 113*).

Choice of fabrics

Stiff materials for making firm lampshades are available at good art and craft shops and at some departmental stores. Keep aware of current trends, and experiment with new products. These are some that make very successful lampshades:

1 Covered lampshade card
Fabric is bonded on to the card, but the range of colours and textures is rather limited. This ready-covered card sometimes involves a certain amount of wastage because of the widths available.

2 Iron-on lampshade card
This is available at craft shops and department stores and is a parchment with an adhesive on one side. Light- to medium-weight fabrics can be successfully applied to this as well as wallpapers and metal foil. The fabric is placed on to the adhesive side and ironed on with a hot iron. The heat releases the adhesive and the fabric sticks firmly to the surface. If using delicate fabrics test a small piece first to make sure it will withstand a hot iron. If not, place a piece of heavier fabric or paper over the cover material before ironing on to the card. Allow the bonded fabric to cool before cutting out the shape required.

3 Selapar
This is a high quality semi-transparent PVC backing 91.5 cm (36 in) wide with an instant adhesion. It can be used with almost all fabrics except open-weave ones. The open part of the fabric catches the dirt and dust which then sticks to the adhesive surface. To use Selapar cut to the size required and press the fabric to the sticky surface, gently peeling off the protective paper as you go (*fig. 114*).

4 White buckram
This is a stiff cloth with a coarse rough weave which gives an interesting texture. It can be tinted or dyed with oils or water colours. It makes a very useful foundation for appliqué, dried flower and other surface decoration (*fig. 115*). When using buckram,

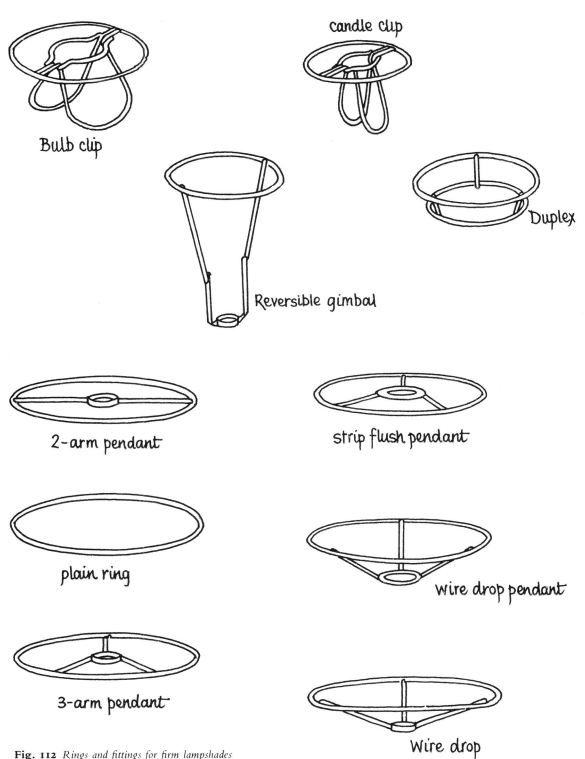

candle clip

Bulb clip

Duplex

Reversible gimbal

2-arm pendant

strip flush pendant

plain ring

wire drop pendant

3-arm pendant

Wire drop

Fig. 112 *Rings and fittings for firm lampshades*

Fig. 113 *Some shapes that can be made using two rings*

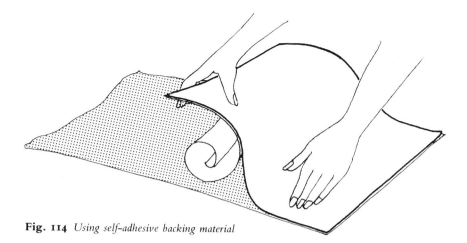

Fig. 114 *Using self-adhesive backing material*

wipe the smooth side with a damp sponge before ironing on the fabric with a hot iron. Cover the fabric with a damp cloth and press again. Allow to dry thoroughly. Embroidery and lace can be applied in this way and if necessary, a little adhesive can be used. Dried flowers and leaves should be applied with adhesive after the foundation material has been sewn to the frame.

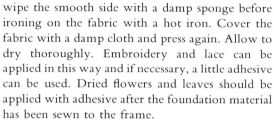

Fig. 115 *Mounting designs on to buckram*

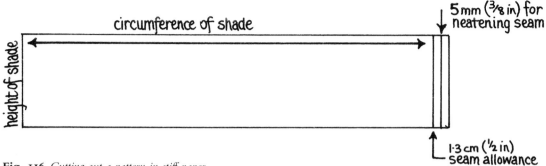

Fig. 116 *Cutting out a pattern in stiff paper*

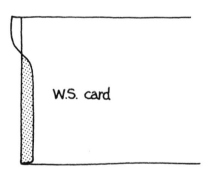

W.S. card

Figs 117 & 118 *Folding the fabric over the card to make a neat edge at the seam*

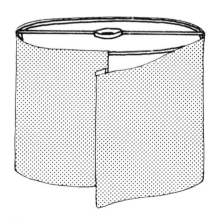

5 *Pelmet buckram*
This is also a useful fabric as its golden brown surface has an interesting texture.

6 *Parchment*
Real parchment in the form of old maps, prints and deeds can also be used successfully provided these are not stained or wrinkled.

When bonding fabric to lampshade card or Selapar cut the fabric 10 mm ($\frac{3}{8}$ in) longer at one short side where the seam allowance is made (*fig. 116*). This should be folded over the cut edge of the card and stuck down to the back of the card with adhesive. It makes a neat edge to the seam and prevents the white edge of the card from showing on the finished lampshade (*figs. 117 and 118*).

Straight-sided drum lampshade

A straight-sided round or oval drum shade is the simplest of firm shades to make, as two rings of exactly the same size are used – one should be plain and the other with a fitting attached. Strutted frames can be used but are not essential since the rigid material forms the shape of the shade. Wooden clip-on clothes pegs with springs are used to hold the fabric in position on the rings or frame while the stitching is worked.

(1) Prepare and bind the rings in the usual way (see page 27). When starting to bind the plain ring, however, secure the end of the tape to the ring with

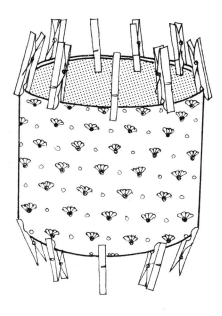

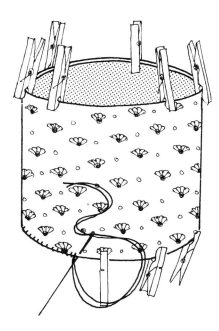

Fig. 119 *Attaching the fabric to the rings with clothes pegs to make a firm lampshade*

Fig. 120 *Sewing the material to the rings with blanket stitch*

a little sticky tape to prevent it from slipping. Finish by over-sewing the tape on the outer edge of the ring so that when the fabric or card is applied to the ring it covers the stitching (*fig. 28*).

(2) To estimate the amount of material required measure round the taped rings to find the circumference of the shade, then decide on the height of the finished lampshade.

(3) Make a pattern using stiff paper, cutting it into a rectangle the required depth (height of the shade) and width (circumference of the shade) plus 1.3 cm ($\frac{1}{2}$ in) for a seam allowance (*fig. 116*).

(4) Fit the pattern on to the rings using wooden clip-on clothes pegs. Check the proportion of the shade and the fit of the pattern and adjust if necessary.

(5) Cut out the fabric carefully, using the paper pattern, and attach it to the rings with the wooden clothes pegs (*fig. 119*).

(6) With a double thread and a strong needle (Betweens 5/6) sew through the fabric to the tape round the top and bottom rings, using a blanket stitch (*fig. 120*). These stitches are covered by the

trimming. Make sure that the fabric does not extend above or below the rings or it will give an unsightly appearance to the finish (*fig. 121*).

(7) Finish sewing 5 cm (2 in) from where the seam is to be positioned at the side of the shade. On the wrong side of the material mark a seam allowance of 6 mm ($\frac{1}{4}$ in), using a ruler and pencil. Trim off the fabric to the pencil line taking care to cut a perfectly straight edge. Alternatively, fold over the 10 mm ($\frac{3}{8}$ in) fabric to the wrong side of the card to make a neat edge (*figs 117 and 118*).

(8) Overlap the seam and apply adhesive evenly to both edges. Press together firmly until the seam is secure. Complete the blanket stitching at the top and bottom ring.

(9) Sewing trimmings on to hard rigid materials is impractical, so apply the trimming to the top and bottom of the shade with an adhesive. Spread this evenly and thinly on to the trimming and then press firmly over the stitches until secure. Turn in the ends of the trimming 1.3 cm ($\frac{1}{2}$ in) and butt them together. Patterns, if any, should be matched if possible.

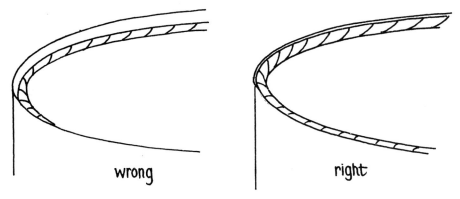

Fig. 121 *Position of fabric on the taped ring*

Cone and coolie lampshades

When making a cone, near-drum or coolie shade in firm fabric (i.e. one that is smaller at the top than at the bottom) it is necessary to make a pattern first, to ensure that the material fits exactly. For a strutted frame use the first method given, but if it is necessary to use a ring set the second method must be employed.

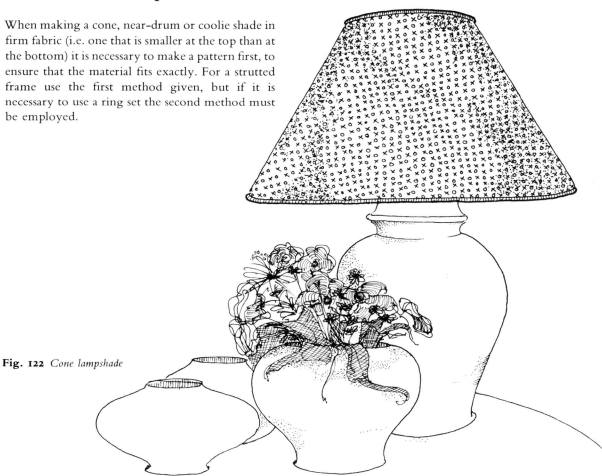

Fig. 122 *Cone lampshade*

Method 1

(1) Prepare and bind the frame in the usual way (see page 27).

(2) Take a large piece of stiff paper and place the taped frame on to it, holding it firmly.

(3) Starting at the side strut, draw along the outside of the strut with a pencil and mark the top and bottom. Rotate the frame slowly, carefully marking along the top and bottom rings until the first strut is reached. Make sure that the frame is held firmly or an accurate pattern will not be obtained. Make a 1.3 cm ($\frac{1}{2}$ in) seam allowance at one end (*fig. 123*).

(4) If a large shade is required the pattern can be taken from one half of the frame only, and the lampshade made with two pieces of material cut from the same pattern. In this case remember to reverse the pattern on the fabric for the second half (*fig. 124*).

Fig. 123 *Taking a pattern for a cone shade*

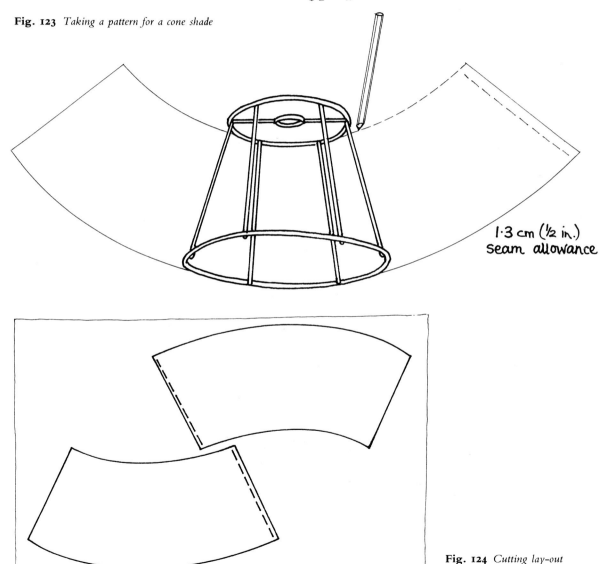

1·3 cm (½ in.) seam allowance

Fig. 124 *Cutting lay-out for a large cone lampshade*

(5) Cut out the pattern, fit on to the frame and adjust if necessary.

(6) Cut out the fabric from the paper pattern and secure to the frame with clothes pegs.

(7) Stitch to the frame and finish as for the straight-sided drum lampshade (see page 64).

Method 2

(1) Make this pattern on a large sheet of graph paper.

(2) Prepare and bind the rings.

(3) Take measurements over the taped rings so that an accurate pattern is obtained (*fig. 125*).
    (a) The height required for the shade.
    (b) The diameter and circumference of the top ring (AB).
    (c) The diameter and circumference of the bottom ring (CD).

(4) On the paper draw a horizontal line CD which is the diameter of the bottom ring (*fig. 126*). At the middle of CD which is X, draw a vertical line from X to Y. This equals the height of the shade. Angle YXD is a right angle of 90 degrees.

(5) Draw a horizontal line through Y making it parallel with CD. AB equals the diameter of the top ring, with AY equal to YB. Join CA and DB and continue these lines until they meet the perpendicular line at Z. If the pattern is accurate the two lines meet at the same point.

(6) With a large compass, using Z as the centre, draw two arcs of circles: the first with radius ZB and the second with radius ZD. Alternatively, use a piece of buckram or card with a drawing pin in one end at Z (*fig. 127*). Make a hole in the buckram or card at the correct point and push a pencil point through it.

(7) First draw the arc from point B round to point E (this is the circumference of the top ring), then draw an arc from point D to point F (this is the circumference of the bottom ring). This gives the size of the shade. Add 6 mm ($\frac{1}{4}$ in) for an overlapping join in the shade.

(8) Join FE and continue the line. This should pass through point Z if the pattern is accurate.

(9) Place a ruler between D and G and mark the centre. From this point place the ruler to Z and mark a grain line.

Fig. 125 *Taking the measurements for a cone or coolie lampshade*

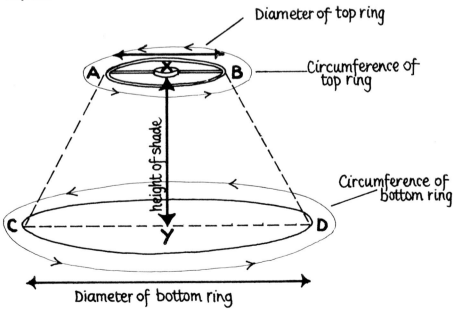

Diameter of top ring

Circumference of top ring

height of shade

Circumference of bottom ring

Diameter of bottom ring

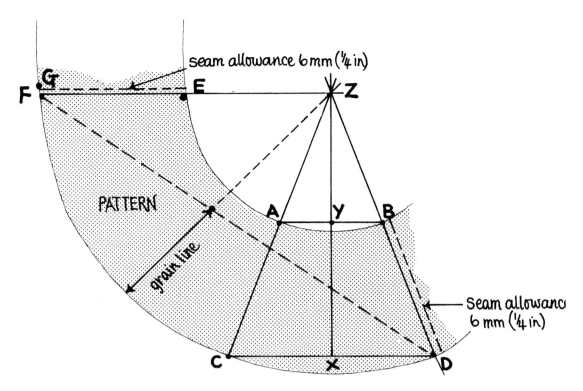

Fig. 126 *Drafting a pattern for a cone or coolie shade (Method 2)*

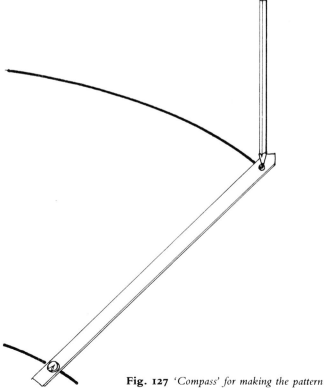

Fig. 127 *'Compass' for making the pattern*

69

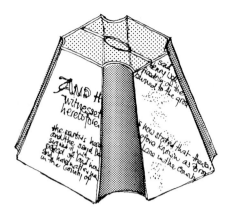

Fig. 128 *A parchment shade with velvet corners*

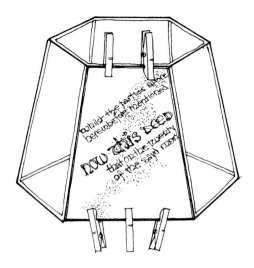

Fig. 131 *Applying the first parchment section to the frame*

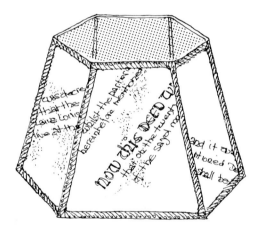

Fig. 129 *A parchment shade using old deeds*

(10) Cut out the pattern and try on the rings. When an accurate pattern has been obtained and the fit is satisfactory, cut out the lampshade fabric using the pattern and noting the grain line.

(11) Make up the shade using the instructions for the straight-sided drum shade (see page 64).

Parchment lampshades

Old deeds and maps are sometimes available from which successful lampshades can be made. This is a particularly interesting way of re-covering frames in traditional materials. Other rigid fabrics can also be used in this way (*figs 128–133*).

(1) Prepare and tape the frame in the usual way (see page 27).

(2) Where each section is the same size make a pattern of one of them using a piece of stiff paper. Draw round the section carefully, adding 6 mm (¼ in) all round. Test the pattern on the lampshade frame and trim and adjust where necessary.

(3) Lay the pattern on to the wrong side of the parchment and draw round, cutting out the number of sections required.

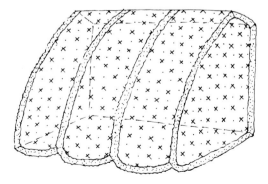

Fig. 130 *Rigid fabric used on a bedhead frame*

(4) Fix the first section to the frame using clip-on clothes pegs to hold it into position (*fig. 131*). If the parchment is not too thick it is best stitched to the frame as for the straight-sided drum (see page 64). However, if the parchment is too thick for stitching apply adhesive round the edges of each side and apply carefully to the outside of the lampshade frame. Press this firmly into position and allow to dry thoroughly before the next section is fixed.

(5) Apply each panel in the same way, overlapping the sections at the side edges.

(6) Cover the stitches or joins at the struts with a suitable braid and apply matching trimming to the top and bottom rings, using adhesive to apply all the trimmings (*fig. 129*).

Velvet or other medium/heavy-weight fabric can be used in conjunction with parchment and this is stitched to the frame as for the sectional shades. Stitch this to the frame first before applying the parchment. The two combinations of materials make an attractive shade (*fig. 128*).

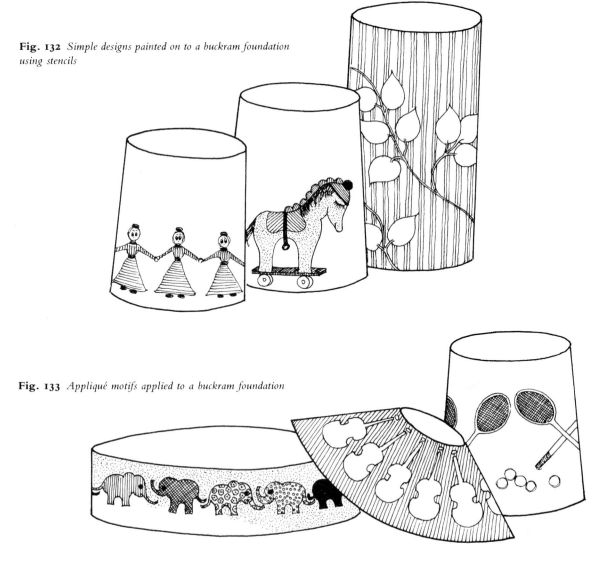

Fig. 132 *Simple designs painted on to a buckram foundation using stencils*

Fig. 133 *Appliqué motifs applied to a buckram foundation*

Pleated paper shades

Attractive, pleated conical shades can be made quite simply, using wallpaper or other substantial papers. Alternatively, fabric or paper can be first applied to Selapar. This gives a more permanent result, but demands a little more patience and accuracy. Pleated shades of this type have enjoyed a revival recently and are best made on conical, strutted frames. Use a plastic-coated frame if possible, as these do not need to be taped when making this type of lampshade.

Estimate the amount of paper required by measuring twice the circumference of the lower ring. This makes the most effective pleating. (If necessary, the paper or Selapar can be joined to give the necessary measurement of the circumference of the frame.) Make the join, after pleating the paper or Selapar, by overlapping the ends of the paper and securing with adhesive so that the join is concealed inside a pleat. The depth of the paper should be the length of the side strut of the frame plus 2.5 cm (1 in) at the top edge and 2.5 cm (1 in) at the lower edge.

(1) Cut out the paper or Selapar to the required size.

(2) On the wrong side, and working from the top to the bottom of the paper, measure and mark out with a pencil accurate guide lines for the pleating. 1.9 cm ($\frac{3}{4}$ in) is usually a suitable measurement for most sizes of shade, but this can be varied to suit individual requirements.

(3) Draw a guide line 2.5 cm (1 in) down from the top edge on the wrong side using a faint pencil line. This marks the position of holes which need to be punched in each pleat along the top edge, through which to thread ribbon or cord. This is then drawn up to fit the top ring.

(4) Fold the paper carefully making concertina-like pleats, following the guide lines on the wrong side of the paper. Make any joins necessary, overlapping the edges so that they are concealed in a pleat. Secure with a good adhesive.

(5) Punch a hole in the centre of each pleat using the guide lines 2.5 cm (1 in) from the top edge (see 3 above). Thread a length of cord or narrow ribbon through the holes and draw up the top edge until it fits snugly over the top of the frame. Make sure that the pleats are arranged evenly around the frame and tie a knot or a bow to secure.

3 Pleated chiffon makes a traditional style of shade

4 Conical shade made from firm fabric

5 Tiffany-style lampshade in a country kitchen

6 Pleated paper covers a conical shade

7 Cone lampshade using furnishing fabric

8 A perfect balance gives an elegant result

EIGHT
Trimmings

Trimming is used on a lampshade to cover stitches and sometimes seams, but it also serves to decorate and complement the finished shade.

Careful consideration should be given to the texture of the fabric and the style of the lampshade, as well as to the base on which it will stand. If the lampshade is of a traditional design made in fine silk then a silky trimming would be suitable. If, on the other hand, the shade is made from a coarsely woven or rigid fabric and is intended for a pottery base, then a thicker cotton braid or one with a matt finish would be more appropriate. Always relate the trimming to the base and to the fabric as well as to the colour. Keep silky braids and fringes for soft silky shades and use thicker, more coarsely woven trimmings for cotton fabrics and firm lampshades. These more closely match the firmer texture of these materials.

If an exact colour match cannot be found use a contrasting colour or one that is used to decorate some other item of soft furnishing in the room, providing the colours work well together.

Beware of using fussy trimmings; these usually do not enhance a lampshade. Consider instead the plainer and more tailored braids and trimmings, which give the lampshade a professional-looking finish. They are often less costly than more elaborate trimmings and are more elegant.

Although there is a wide range of attractive, commercially made trimmings in many widths and styles, it is not always easy to match colours exactly. If colours cannot be matched and a contrast is not possible, gold and silver metallic braids and laces can be used; they work well with many colours and fabrics and can also be used successfully with some hand-made trimmings (e.g. crossway strip).

Hand-made trimmings can be made using bobbin lace, crochet, tatting or macramé techniques, or by plaiting braids, wools or rushes in various thicknesses. Velvet ribbon can be most effective, either used plain or gathered and applied to the top and bottom edges of a shade. Machine embroidery can also be used to advantage to make scalloped edges. A petal-edged ruching can be made by working diagonal rows of small running stitches on a folded crossway strip (*figs 146–148*).

Fashions in trimmings change, so keep aware of current trends by looking at good lighting departments to note any details of interest. Remember that a lampshade can be spoilt by the wrong choice of decoration.

Types of trimming

1 Lampshade braid

This is a loosely woven braid found in many textures, colours and patterns, and is usually made from cotton or rayon. It is especially designed for use with lampshades and should not be confused with upholstery gimp which is less flexible and more closely woven than lampshade braid and is not therefore suitable for trimming shades as it does not mould easily to a curve.

2 Rayon/silk bobble fringe

This is mostly made from silk or rayon and interspersed with small wooden balls covered in silk. It is rather costly.

3 Cotton bobble fringe

Similar to the above but less costly as the bobbles are made from compressed cotton. White bobble fringe

Fig. 134 *Russia braid combines well with a crossway strip*

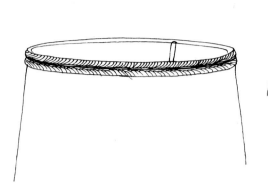

can be dyed quite easily at home if a suitable colour cannot be obtained.

4 Tassel fringe
Usually made from silk or rayon. The fringe is made in various depths and is interspersed with tassels of various sizes.

5 Fringing
A plain fringe made from rayon or cotton in many depths and thicknesses. Can be a cut or a looped fringe. Cotton fringing is easily dyed at home.

6 Russia braid
An artificial silk cord which can be combined successfully with a strip of fabric cut on the cross (*fig. 134*). Particularly attractive in a lurex finish.

7 Metallic braids and laces
These make very attractive trimmings but because of their openwork texture a crossway strip or velvet ribbon needs to be used with them to conceal the stitching on the top and bottom rings of the lampshade. Most of them wash well. The colours tend to mellow with use but this is not unattractive.

8 Velvet ribbon
A most useful form of trimming as it looks effective on both delicate lampshades or on coarse firm lampshades. However, as it will not stretch easily and mould to a curve it is not suitable for all types of shades, particularly those with well-defined curves. When possible, use narrow width ribbon (10 mm [$\frac{3}{8}$ in]). Wider widths of ribbon can be gathered up to make more elaborate trimmings.

9 Miscellaneous trimmings
Other types of trimmings can be used for decorating lampshades. These include piping cord (*fig. 135*), appliqué, patchwork, crochet, and bobbin lace.

Application of trimmings

Measure accurately the circumference of the top and bottom rings to estimate the amount of trimming required. Add 5 cm (2 in) to each measurement. This allows 1.3 cm ($\frac{1}{2}$ in) turnings and a little extra to enable the trimming to be eased on to the shade. A trimming should always be sewn on to the lampshade unless a more even effect can be achieved by using an adhesive – i.e. when using narrow velvet ribbon, Russia braid or crossway strip.

When applying trimmings make sure that the two joins at the top and bottom of the lampshade are made on the same side of the shade.

1 Braids and fringes
Fold in the end of the trimming 1.3 cm ($\frac{1}{2}$ in) and if it frays, secure the end with a little adhesive. Starting at a side strut pin on the trimming and sew as in figs 136 and 137 using a zig-zag type stitch, taking a stitch at the top and bottom of the trimming alternately. Take care that the stitching does not go through to the inside of the shade. Finish off by turning in the end of the trimming 1.3 cm ($\frac{1}{2}$ in) and

Fig. 135 *Piping cord used to decorate a firm shade*

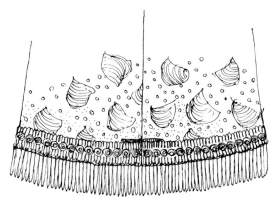

Fig. 138 *The ends of the braid butted together*

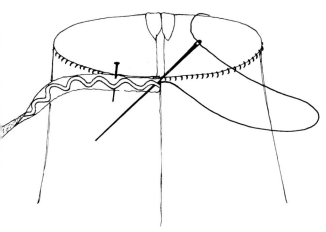

Fig. 136 *Sewing on a braid with a zig-zag stitch*

butt the two ends together (*fig. 138*). Match any pattern, if possible, and slipstitch the edges together afterwards. The trimming should be eased on to the shade and not stretched. When sewing on a bobble fringe or any other type of fringing beware of sewing too tightly. Tight stitches will pull the trimming to the inside of the bottom ring of the shade and the fringing will not hang well. When applying braid to half and three-quarter shades make sure the join in the trimming is made in the most inconspicuous place. This is usually at the lower edge.

2 Velvet ribbons

As these lack elasticity they need to be stretched on to the shade and secured with an adhesive. Butt the ends in the same way as 1 above but do not slip stitch together. By sticking rather than sewing this trimming to the shade a more even result is achieved.

3 Crossway strip

This is an excellent, inexpensive way of covering stitches and seams on many styles of lampshade; carefully applied, it gives very good results. Make it in the same fabric or colour as the lampshade itself to cover seams on tiffany and other shades. It is less conspicuous than commercially made braids and moulds very well over curves. However, fabrics that do not fold and press well are not suitable.

Follow the instructions for the cutting and preparation of the strip on page 81.

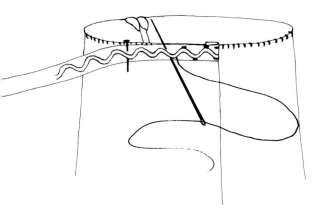

Fig. 137 *Sewing on the trimming. The long stitch is hidden between the braid and the shade*

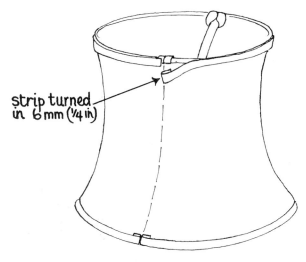

strip turned
in 6 mm (¼ in)

Fig. 139 *Positioning the joins at the same side of the shade*

(a) When attaching this strip to the top and bottom of a shade apply the end of it to the outside edge of the shade starting 6 mm ($\frac{1}{4}$ in) beyond a strut. The strip should just cover the oversewing stitches but should not extend to the inside of the shade. To finish off, turn in 6 mm ($\frac{1}{4}$ in) at the end of the strip, secure with a little adhesive and apply over the starting end (*fig. 65*). Make sure that the joins at the top and bottom rings are positioned on the same side of the shade (*fig. 139*).

(b) To neaten struts with crossway strip cut and prepare strips 3.2 cm ($1\frac{1}{4}$ in) wide and the length of the strut plus 2.5 cm (1 in). Fold into three to make a strip approximately 1.3 cm ($\frac{1}{2}$ in) wide (*fig. 63*).

(c) Apply adhesive to the wrong side of one end of the strip and secure it to the top ring. Place a pin at the top ring to hold the strip firmly in position whilst the rest of the strip is applied. Stretch the strip slightly and position it over the stitching on the strut. Press it firmly to the shade with the fingers making sure it adheres firmly to the shade. Apply the strip two or three centimeters (inches) at a time so that a perfectly even finish is achieved. Put a pin at the bottom ring to hold the strip firmly until the adhesive has dried thoroughly (*see fig. 64*).

Hand-made trimmings

Hand-made trimmings can be made using crochet, tatting or macramé techniques, or by plaiting braids, wools or rushes in various thicknesses. The same careful thought is necessary when choosing and making these as when selecting commercially made trimmings. They should be similar in weight and texture to the outer cover of the shade and must be dense enough to cover the stitching.

1 Tatting, crochet, bobbin lace, embroidery, macramé
These can all be used successfully for trimming lampshades. Remember to use a suitable thickness of thread. Decorative trimmings can be made with automatic sewing machines using built-in embroidery stitches and twin needles. If chosen and executed with care these trimmings can be most effective (*fig. 140*). If necessary, use a strip of light-weight vilene or bonding fabric to neaten the raw edges.

2 Gathered velvet ribbon
This is a particularly suitable trimming for a lampshade with a collar. Insert a small roll of synthetic wadding or cotton wool underneath the gathered velvet ribbon to give it a padded effect.

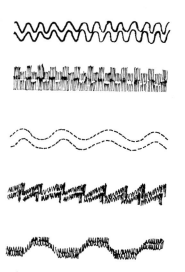

Fig. 140 *Some machine embroidery stitches make attractive trimmings*

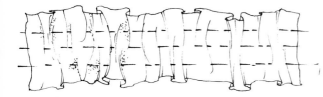

Fig. 141 *Gathering velvet ribbon*

Use twice the circumference of the ring and make one, two or three rows of running stitches depending on the width of the ribbon. Gather up and attach to the shade with adhesive (*figs 141 and 142*).

3 Patchwork motifs

These can be used successfully on lampshades to trim round the top and bottom rings. If necessary they can be mounted first on to a strip of ribbon so that they are easier to handle (*figs. 143 and 144*).

Fig. 142 *Insert synthetic wadding underneath velvet ribbon to achieve a padded effect*

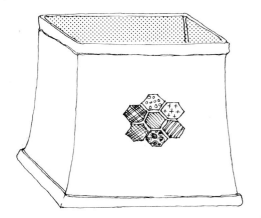

Fig. 143 *Ideas for lampshades using patchwork motifs*

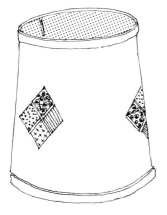

Fig. 144 *Border patterns made in patchwork*

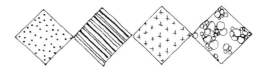

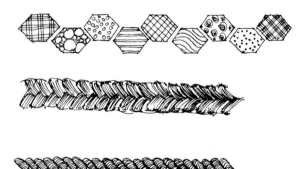

5 Petal-edged ruching

(a) Cut out and prepare a crossway strip the width required (usually 1.3–2.5 cm [½–1 in]). (See page 81.)

(b) Measure and mark 2.5 cm (1 in) points along the fabric as in fig. 146. Work diagonal rows of small running stitches on the right side of the material (fig. 147).

(c) Draw up the work and apply to the lampshade with an adhesive (fig. 148).

Fig. 145 *Plaited rushes and braids make effective trimmings*

4 Plaiting

Russia braid looks effective when plaited and this is available in a lurex finish as well as in many colours. Rushes can be plaited and used on firm lampshades as their texture admirably suits this type of shade. Plaited knitting wools and twines in various thicknesses also make pleasing trimmings for firm lampshades (fig. 145).

Fig. 148 *Petal-edged ruching*

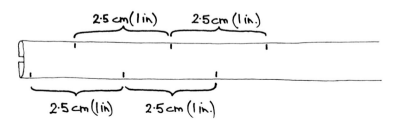

Fig. 146 *Marking points for a petal-edged ruching*

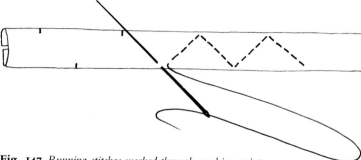

Fig. 147 *Running stitches worked through marking points*

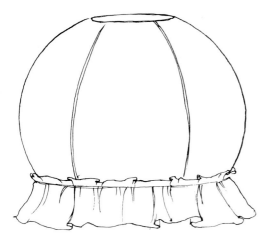

Fig. 149 *Gathered frill on a tiffany-style lampshade*

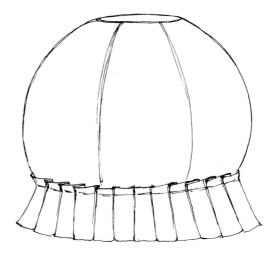

Fig. 150 *Pleated frill on a tiffany-style lampshade*

6 Chiffon

When making pleated chiffon or georgette lampshades tear or cut off the selvedge before preparing the fabric for pleating. This is ideal for covering the stitches round the top and bottom rings before another trimming is applied. Turn in the raw edge and secure to the shade with small stitches or an adhesive.

7 Frills

A gathered or pleated frill is an attractive way of decorating some styles of lampshades, particularly the tiffany styles. The frill varies in size and construction depending on the shade and the fabric. When using thin, lightweight fabrics use double frills as they give a more pleasing result.

Single frill

(a) To make a frill with single fabric, cut a strip on the straight grain 7.5–10.0 cm (3–4 in) wide and one and a half to twice the circumference of the bottom ring. Join the short ends of the strip together with a narrow French seam.

(b) For the lower edge of the frill make a hem by turning in the long sides 6 mm (¼ in) and machine in position with a small zig-zag stitch (*fig. 151*).

(c) At the top edge of the frill turn in the raw edge 1.9 cm (¾ in) along the other long side. Work a row of running stitches along this edge 1.3 cm (½ in)

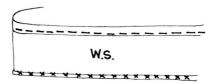

Fig. 151 *Neatening the top and lower edges of a single frill*

Fig. 152 *Joining the two short ends of the strip with a flat seam*

from the top (*fig. 151*). Gather up the stitches and pin into position. Adjust to fit the bottom ring of the lampshade. Secure the frill with adhesive.

Double frill

(a) To make a double frill cut a piece of fabric on the straight grain 10–15 cm (4–6 in) wide and one and a half to twice the circumference of the bottom ring.

(b) Join the two short ends of the strip with a flat seam and press open (*fig. 152*).

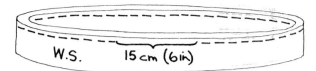

Fig. 153 *Stitching the frill leaving an opening of 15 cm (6 in)*

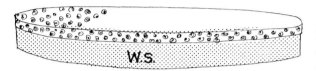

Fig. 154 *Position of seam on wrong side of frill*

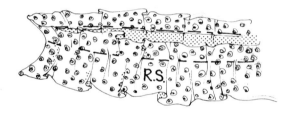

Fig. 155 *Working a gathering stitch round the top edge of the frill*

Pleated frill

Cut out and prepare the strips of fabric as for the double or single frill, but allow three times the circumference of the bottom ring of the lampshade. Make the frill in the same way as for the gathered frill, but pin into small pleats, measuring each one accurately so that the finished pleating measures the same as the circumference of the bottom ring (*fig. 156*). Tack and press. To hold the pleats into position work two rows of machine stitching 3 mm ($\frac{1}{8}$ in) apart and 1.3 cm ($\frac{1}{2}$ in) from the top edge of the frill (*fig. 158*). Pin the frill to the bottom ring of the lampshade and secure with small stitches or an adhesive. A narrow velvet ribbon or other trimming could be applied to cover the machine stitching.

Figs 156, 157 & 158 *Making a pleated frill*

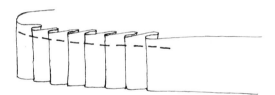

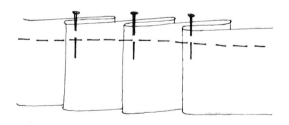

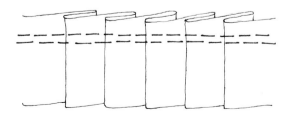

(c) Fold the frill in half lengthwise with right sides together and stitch as in fig. 153 leaving an opening approximately 15 cm (6 in) long.

(d) Turn the right side outside through the opening and slipstitch the opening by hand. Press the tube so that the seam is approximately 1.3 cm ($\frac{1}{2}$ in) from the top edge on the wrong side of the frill (*fig. 154*).

(e) Work a running stitch round the top edge of the frill near the seam line, taking the stitching through both layers of fabric (*fig. 155*).

(f) Gather up the stitches and pin into position to fit round the bottom ring of the lampshade. Adjust the gathers evenly and secure with adhesive.

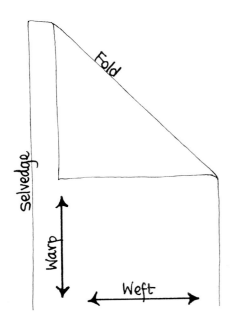

Fig. 159 *Folding the fabric to find the cross grain*

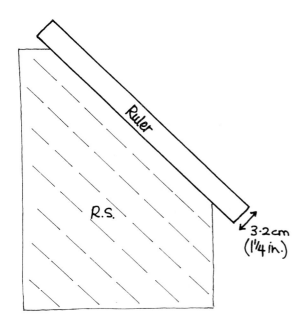

Fig. 160 *Marking parallel lines on the fabric with a rigid rule*

8 Crossway strip

This is a useful trimming for lampshades and is most economical as it can often be made from left-over pieces of fabric. It is easy to make, and when well executed gives a tailored, professional finish to a lampshade. Use it to cover stitches and seams. It also looks effective when used with other trimmings such as metallic laces and narrow braids.

Cutting fabric on the cross
(1) Fold the material diagonally so that the selvedge thread lies across the crossways thread, i.e. the warp across the weft (*fig. 159*). Press. Cut along the fold. The material is then on the true bias or cross grain.

(2) In order to make all the strips the same size, make a ruler in stiff card 3.2 cm (1¼ in) wide to use as a guide. This is the most suitable size of strip for trimming lampshades.

(3) Place the edge of the ruler to the cut edge of the fabric and mark with a sharp piece of tailors' chalk, making parallel lines the same width. Cut along the lines. Continue in this way until sufficient strips have been made (*fig. 160*).

(4) Fold the lengths in three and press to make a crossway strip approximately 1.3 cm (½ in) wide (*fig. 161*).

Fig. 161 *Folding the strip to make it approximately 1.3 cm (½ in) wide*

(5) If joining the strips together to fit round the top or bottom of a lampshade always make the join on the straight grain of the fabric (*fig. 162*). Place the two strips together with right sides facing, and pin and stitch the seam with a small machine or backstitch, making sure that the strips form an angle as shown in fig. 162. Press the seam open and trim away the corners (*fig. 163*).

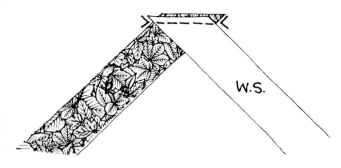

Fig. 162 *Joining crossway strips on the straight grain*

Fig. 163 *The seam pressed open*

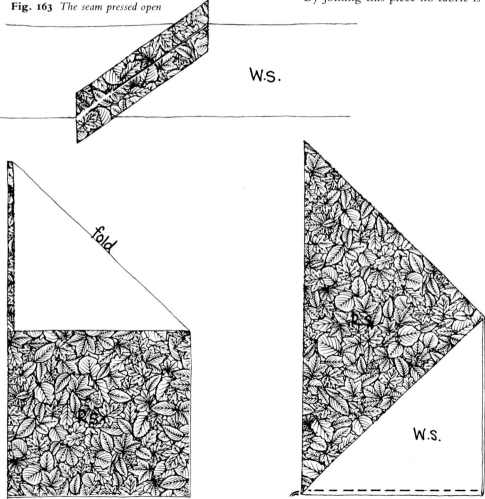

Quick method of cutting on the cross

If large amounts of crossway strip are required it is useful to be able to make it without having to join each strip separately. The following simple method can save many hours of work and can also be used successfully in soft furnishings.

(1) Take a strip of fabric 23 cm (9 in) wide. The length of the strip should be at least twice the width i.e. 46 cm (18 in) or more.

(2) Fold over the top right-hand corner to obtain the direct cross (*fig. 164*). Cut off this corner and join to the lower edge with a 6 mm ($\frac{1}{4}$ in) seam (*fig. 165*). By joining this piece no fabric is wasted.

Fig. 164 *Folding the fabric to obtain the true bias*

Fig. 165 *Cut off corner joined to the lower edge*

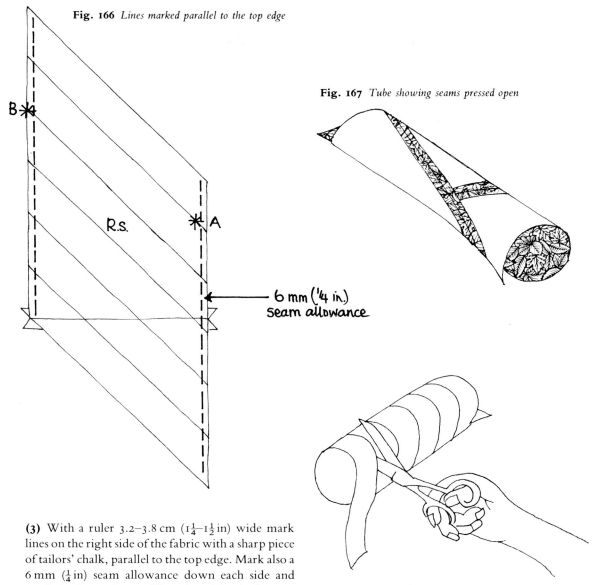

Fig. 166 *Lines marked parallel to the top edge*

B

R.S.

A

6 mm (¼ in.)
seam allowance

Fig. 167 *Tube showing seams pressed open*

Fig. 168 *Cutting the crossway strip*

(3) With a ruler 3.2–3.8 cm (1¼–1½ in) wide mark lines on the right side of the fabric with a sharp piece of tailors' chalk, parallel to the top edge. Mark also a 6 mm (¼ in) seam allowance down each side and mark the first and second lines A and B as in fig. 166.

(4) Take a pin through the wrong side of the fabric at point A and take this across to point B, pinning very accurately with right sides together. Continue pinning along the seam. Tack and stitch the seam, checking first that the lines match up exactly. This makes a tube. Press the seam open (*fig. 167*).

(5) Turn to the right side and start cutting round the tube at the projecting strip at the top edge (*fig. 168*).

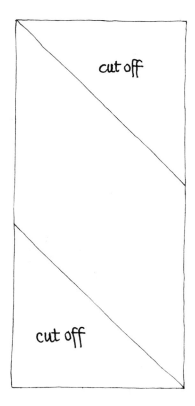

Fig. 169 *Alternative method of cutting fabric*

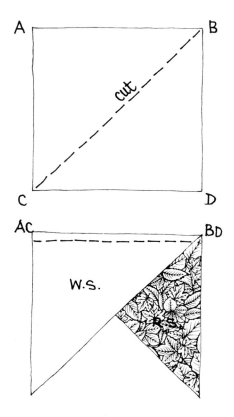

Fig. 170 *Using a square piece of fabric*

A length of 23 cm ($\frac{1}{4}$ yd) of fabric 91.5 cm (36 in) wide makes approximately 5 m (5$\frac{1}{2}$ yds) of crossway strip 3.8 cm (1$\frac{1}{2}$ in) wide.

If larger pieces of fabric are available the top right-hand corner and the bottom left-hand corner can be cut off and set aside. This produces the same shaped piece of fabric but has the advantage of

having fewer joins in the tube. Remember that the length of the strip of fabric must be at least twice the width (*fig. 169*).

Square pieces of fabric can be utilised in a similar way by cutting and joining as in fig. 170 placing AB to CD with right sides together.

NINE
Ideas for covering bases

Old bases can be given a new lease of life quite successfully by covering them with fabric or other decorative material such as felt, hessian, paper etc. Alternatively, blocks of wood or even bricks, jars and vases can be covered in the same way and made into lamp bases.

(1) Make a pattern of the base in paper (*fig. 172*) and test over the base. When the fit is perfect cut out the fabric or other material using the paper pattern and apply to the base using a good adhesive.

(2) Neaten the seams with lampshade trimming or upholstery gimp (*fig. 173*). Alternatively, a piece of crossway strip can be used if the fabric is suitable.

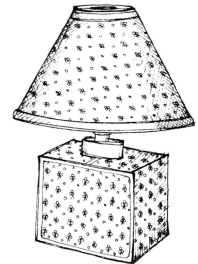

Fig. 171 *Covering a base with fabric*

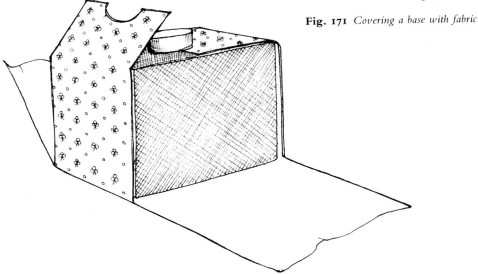

Fig. 172 *Making a pattern of the base in paper*

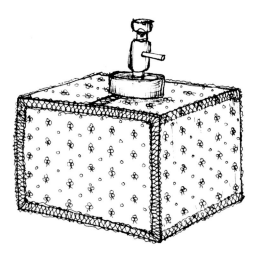

Fig. 173 *Neaten the seams with upholstery gimp or other decorative trimming*

Fig. 175 *Cut-out shapes of moons and stars decorate both lampshade and base*

Fig. 174 *Postage stamps or small decorative cards make an interesting scheme for both lampshade and base*

(3) The base can be decorated with postage stamps, colourful small cards or stickers, or date sheets of small calendars. These could also be applied to the lampshade to make a co-ordinating base and shade (*figs. 174 and 175*).

(4) Cord can also be used effectively to decorate a lampshade base. Use a thick piping cord or decorative cotton furnishing cord. Coil the cord to form a base and then stick it to the bottom of the base with a good adhesive. Wind the cord round the lampbase applying adhesive both on the cord and the base, finishing off neatly at the top (*fig. 176*). Secure firmly with adhesive. When this has dried thoroughly the base can be varnished or painted with gloss or enamel paint (use an undercoat first). Match the lampshade to the base by trimming it with the same cord as used on the base (*fig. 177*).

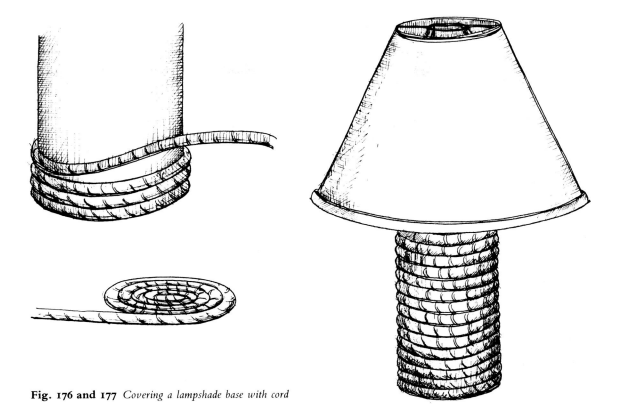

Fig. 176 and 177 *Covering a lampshade base with cord*

TEN
Care of lampshades

Lampshades can be kept looking fresh and clean by regular brushing with a soft brush. Make sure that any trimming is treated carefully.

Most soft lampshades wash well if care is taken. It is important to dry the shade as quickly as possible to prevent the frame rusting, although many frames are now treated with a plastic coating which obviates this problem. Choose a good drying day and wash the shade gently in warm water, using a mild liquid detergent (*fig. 178*). Rinse thoroughly and hang on the line to drip dry (*fig. 179*).

To ensure that the shade is perfectly dry put it in an airing cupboard for twenty-four hours (*fig. 180*). This also helps the fabric to tighten up on the frame. Washing can sometimes improve a shade that is loose and baggy, as the fabric tends to shrink a little and this makes the lampshade tighter.

If coloured trimmings have been used on the lampshade check their colour fastness before washing the shade.

As most firm or rigid shades cannot be washed because of their paper content they should be kept clean by regular brushing with a soft brush. Some can be sponged clean, but this depends on the materials used.

If a finger is pricked accidentally when the lampshade is being made blood can be removed from the fabric by chewing a piece of tacking thread and rubbing it gently on the bloodstain. This sucessfully removes the stain without leaving a water mark.

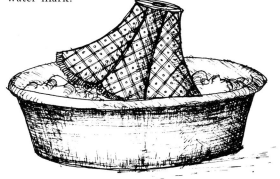

Fig. 178 *Wash lampshades carefully in warm water using a gentle liquid detergent. If necessary, use the bath for larger shades*

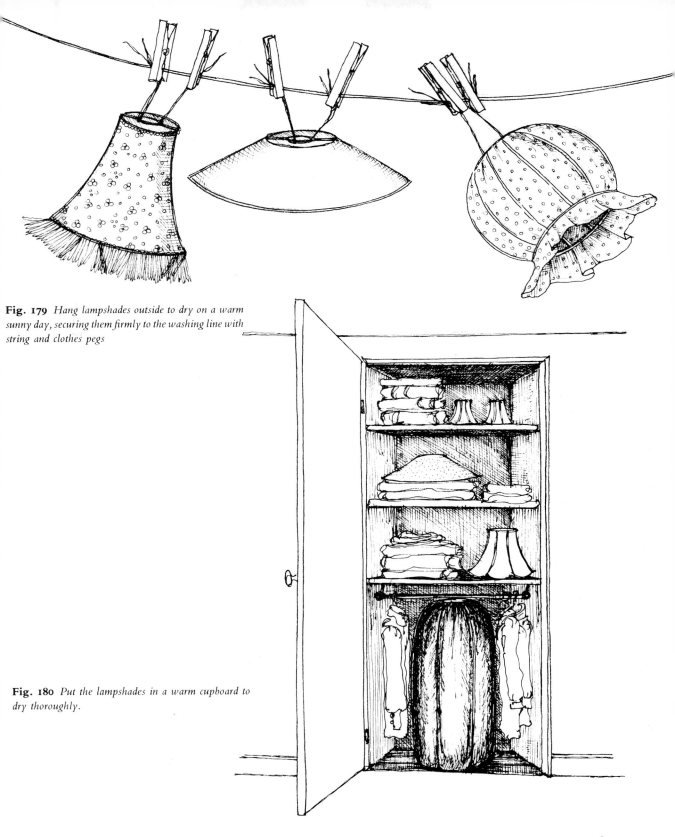

Fig. 179 *Hang lampshades outside to dry on a warm sunny day, securing them firmly to the washing line with string and clothes pegs*

Fig. 180 *Put the lampshades in a warm cupboard to dry thoroughly.*

Suppliers and useful addresses

U.K.

John Lewis
Oxford St
London W1 and branches
Frames, fabrics, tape, trimmings

Laura Ashley
183 Sloane St
London SW1 and branches
Fabrics, trimmings

Arthur Sanderson & Sons Ltd
Sanderson House
Berners St
London W1
Fabrics

Distinctive Trimmings
11 Marylebone Lane
London W1 and
17 Church St
London W8
Trimmings

M. and F. Products (Croydon) Ltd
Wandle Mills
Bridle Path
Beddington
Croydon, Surrey
Frames, fabrics for firm lampshades, trimmings
(Write for details of nearest stockists)

McCullach & Wallis Ltd
25–26 New Bond St
London W1
Fabrics, haberdashery

Rufflette Ltd
Sharston Rd
Wythenshawe
Manchester
Trimmings
(Write for details of nearest stockists)

Russell Trading Co.
75 Paradise St
Liverpool
Fabrics, trimmings, tape
(Mail order)

U.S.A.

Georgetown Printworks
1655 Wisconsin Avenue NW
Washington DC 20007
Frames, fabrics, trimmings

Nannies Attic
1511 Wisconsin Avenue NW
Washington DC
Fabrics, trimmings

Erica Wilson Needle Works
717 Madison Avenue
New York

Chain stores:
Ben Franklin Stores
Jefferson Stores
MH Lamston
Sears Roebuck
Woolworths

The American Crafts Council
29 West 53rd Street
New York

Gives information about craft organizations and courses

Glossary

British terms and their American counterparts

airing cupboard – airing closet where linens are dried.

appliqué – pieces of fabric or felt applied to another fabric.

balloon lining – a lining that conceals the struts and framework of the lampshade.

binding tape – a special soft loosely woven cotton tape for binding the frame of the lampshade.

broderie anglaise – cotton or cotton/polyester fabric with cut-out embroidery designs.

buckram – stiff cotton or linen cloth with a rough weave.

chandelier fitting – a group of small lights.

crossway strip – bias strip – a strip of fabric cut across the weft and the warp of the fabric.

electrical points – electrical outlets.

external lining – a lining fitted on to the outer side of the struts of the lampshade.

felt – a non-woven fabric that does not fray.

firm lampshades – those made from stiff or rigid materials.

gimbal fitting – a fitting enabling the lampshade to be either fixed to a base or hang from the ceiling.

hessian – coarse sacking; burlap.

pelmet buckram – coarse canvas impregnated with glue.

pendant fitting – a lampshade fitting enabling the shade to hang from the ceiling.

Selapar – high quality semi-transparent PVC backing with instant adhesion, used for making firm lampshades.

selvedge – the edges of a woven fabric running parallel to the warp.

tacking cotton – basting thread.

template – a pattern used as a guide when cutting out.

turnings – seam allowance.

Bibliography

Anne Butler, *Machine Stitches*, Batsford, 1976

Averil Colby, *Patchwork*, Batsford, 1978

Averil Colby, *Quilting*, Batsford, 1976

Angela Fishburn, *The Batsford Book of Soft Furnishings*, Batsford, 1978

Angela Fishburn, *The Batsford Book of Home Furnishings*, Batsford, 1982

Angela Fishburn, *Lampshades Technique and Design*, Batsford, 1975

Angela Fishburn, *Curtains and Window Treatments*, Batsford 1982

David Hicks, *Decoration with Fabrics*, Weidenfeld and Nicolson, 1971

David Hicks, *Living with Design*, Weidenfeld and Nicolson, 1979

Jean Kimmond, *Coats Book of Lacecrafts*, Batsford, 1978

Edward Miller, *Textiles: Properties and Behaviour*, Batsford, 1973

Pamela Nottingham, *Technique of Torchon Lace*, Batsford, 1979

Derek Phillips, *Lighting*, Macdonald and Co. Ltd with the Council of Industrial Design, 1966

Eirian Short, *Quilting, Technique, Design and Application*, Batsford, 1981

Eirian Short, *Introducing Macramé*, Batsford, 1974

Metric conversion table

Inches to centimetres

in	cm	in	cm	in	cm
$\frac{1}{8}$	0.3	10	25.5	30	76.0
$\frac{1}{4}$	0.6	$10\frac{1}{2}$	26.5	31	78.5
$\frac{3}{8}$	1.0	11	28.0	32	81.5
$\frac{1}{2}$	1.3	$11\frac{1}{2}$	29.0	33	84.0
$\frac{3}{4}$	1.9	12	30.5	34	86.5
1	2.5	$12\frac{1}{2}$	31.5	35	89.0
$1\frac{1}{4}$	3.2	13	33.0	36	91.5
$1\frac{1}{2}$	3.8	$13\frac{1}{2}$	34.5	37	94.0
2	5.0	14	35.5	38	96.5
$2\frac{1}{2}$	6.4	$14\frac{1}{2}$	37.0	39	99.0
3	7.5	15	38.0	40	101.5
$3\frac{1}{2}$	9.0	16	40.5		
4	10.0	17	43.0		
$4\frac{1}{2}$	11.5	18	45.5	48	122.0
5	12.5	19	48.5	54	137.0
$5\frac{1}{2}$	14.0	20	51.0		
6	15.0	21	53.5		
$6\frac{1}{2}$	16.5	22	56.0		
7	18.0	23	58.5		
$7\frac{1}{2}$	19.0	24	61.0		
8	20.5	25	63.5		
$8\frac{1}{2}$	21.5	26	66.0		
9	23.0	27	68.5		
$9\frac{1}{2}$	24.0	28	71.0		
		29	73.5		

Index